EMPOWERING COUPLES

Creative Pastoral Care and Counseling Series
Howard W. Stone, Editor

Books in the Series

CREATIVE PASTORAL CARE AND COUNSELING SERIES

EMPOWERING COUPLES

A Narrative Approach to Spiritual Care

Duane R. Bidwell

FORTRESS PRESS   MINNEAPOLIS

For Karee

whose patient love informs each page

EMPOWERING COUPLES
A Narrative Approach to Spiritual Care

Unless otherwise noted, scripture quotations are from the New Revised Standard Version Bible, copyright © 1989 by the Division of Christian Education of the National Council of Churches of Christ in the USA, and are used with permission.

Cover image: Couple at the Beach © iStockphoto.com / Michelle Gibson
Cover design: Tory Herman

Library of Congress Cataloging-in-Publication Data is available
ISBN 978-0-8006-6342-1

The paper used in this publication meets the minimum requirements of American National Standard for Information Sciences—Permanence of Paper for Printed Library Materials, ANSI Z329.48-1984.

Manufactured in the U.S.A.

17   16   15   14   13   1   2   3   4   5   6   7   8   9   10

CONTENTS

EDITOR'S FOREWORD

I married fifty years ago. I am not married to the same woman I married in 1963. She has changed in many ways over these five decades, and so have I. Our marriage is remarkably different from when we were teenagers saying our marriage vows. I like the changes in our relationship, but they have not been without pain. Couple relationships can be difficult; witness the close to 50 percent divorce rate among those who are married.

Being married or in a committed relationship certainly has changed over the last four or five generations. People get married for different reasons now than then: love or emotional satisfaction was not a primary reason long ago; more likely couples were married for social or economical reasons. What constitutes a committed relationship today has changed over the years, and couples have struggled to keep up with the changes in society. Today partners frequently expect each other to provide intimate companionship that fills their spiritual, emotional, social, and sexual needs, even though marriages can rarely meet such high expectations.

Empowering Couples is written for pastoral caregivers and others who offer help to couples. It presents concrete ways in which respectful care can be offered to those in committed relationships. Duane Bidwell, who has served as both parish pastor and now seminary professor, assumes that most couples who come to spiritual caregivers for help do not need some sort of long-term couple or marriage and family therapy. Rather, he believes that most couples can benefit from anywhere from three to seven brief conversations. The task of the spiritual caregiver is to help them get "'unstuck,' on their feet, and back on track" (see the introduction, below).

Bidwell knows that couples have problems but assumes they have strengths as well. A task of the spiritual caregiver is to assist the pair to recognize these strengths and build on them. In the second half of the book, he describes five tasks that can help couples become empowered in their relationships:

- separating people problems and passions,
- mapping mutual influence,
- attending to teamwork,
- reclaiming partnership, and
- telling a new story.

Empowering Couples is not a book on marital therapy. Instead, it presents a way for spiritual caregivers to converse with couples; it is that narrative between couple and caregiver, and within the couple relationship, that is important. As Bidwell points out in his introduction, "My overarching goal with this approach is to allow partners to create a covenant friendship strong enough to resist forces that threaten relationship."

In *Empowering Couples* the author draws from the writings of the desert fathers and mothers of the third to sixth centuries to inform spiritual care to couples. He correlates desert spirituality with narrative therapy and shows how spiritual caregivers can help couples see what "passions" are influencing their relationship negatively and keeping them from loving each other fully. Bidwell uses the couple research of John Gottman to inform his own method of spiritual care, while also drawing from narrative therapy to present a practical way for couples to strengthen their relationships and make them more rewarding.

I am confident that a reading of *Empowering Couples* will strengthen and enrich your spiritual-care ministry. Bidwell brings to his work the wisdom from years of offering and teaching about marriage counseling both in the parish and as a seminary professor. The scope and quality of the care you offer to others is certain to benefit from his knowledge and sound guidance.

Howard W. Stone

Not marital therapy!
but rather marital
Conversation

Introduction

GETTING STARTED: A FRAME FOR WHAT FOLLOWS

Pastor Marc shook his head and sighed. The Kumar-Rands were still arguing as they left his office—and they'd made it clear they wouldn't be back. Three weeks ago, Aisha and Frank confided the tensions in their marriage and asked him for help. Their first two conversations had been difficult, but today's reminded Marc why he tried to avoid counseling couples. He replayed the conversation in his head.

"Marc, tell Frank he's being ridiculous," Aisha implored, interrupting her husband's tirade. "Do you think God intended a husband to treat his wife this way? Do you? I want to know what you think!"

"Yes," Frank added. "I'd like to know what you think, too. This is our third meeting, and you haven't done anything to fix our problem. All you've done is listen and ask questions. What do you think will make our relationship better? Tell us, and tell us fast. I can't take much more of Aisha's whining!"

"Whining? Whining?!" Aisha replied. She turned to Marc. "Do you see how he talks about me, Pastor? Do you see what I have to put up with? Do you see?"

Marc ignored the questions and focused on the couple's relationship, trying hard not to take sides. But Frank eventually exploded: "This is ridiculous! If you're not going to tell us what to do, we're not coming back!" They left immediately.

Marc felt drained, incompetent, and ineffective.

Working with couples can be difficult—and frustrating—for any caregiver. When care is short term, by default or by design, it's particularly challenging to care for couples, navigating change while remaining neutral and focusing on partnership rather than personalities. For these reasons, spiritual caregivers—mental-health professionals; chaplains, imams, rabbis, ministers, and other religious leaders; social workers; and various paid and volunteer caregivers—need a model of caring for couples that is brief, effective, and focused on partnership. That's what this book offers.

This book also offers an approach that is sensitive to the realities encountered by partners. Couples face tremendous pressure today from socioeconomic forces aligned against committed partnerships[1] in North American (and global) contexts. These forces shape relational and intrapersonal dynamics in ways that contribute to, or even cause, the problems that couples experience. Partners can find it difficult to respond in ways that create and maintain positive, "good enough"[2] relationships—that is, partnerships that provide mutual comfort, support, and safety while allowing for independence, growth, and new possibilities, both for the couple together and for each partner as an individual. That's where trained caregivers—spiritual, psychological, social—can lend assistance.

Couples who receive appropriate, empowering guidance from someone who cares (both about the partnership and about the individuals involved) can make significant progress toward resolving their own problems and maintaining a good-enough relationship despite tough times. Many troubled couples do not, in fact, need long-term marriage and family therapy or ongoing, professional intervention. Instead, they benefit from a few conversations with a trusted guide—conversations that empower them to take action, get "unstuck," on their feet, and back on track.

This book equips spiritual caregivers for such conversations. By practicing and mastering five tasks, caregivers can help couples become empowered for significant change. (The degree of change depends, of course, on the couple and the couple's situation, but in many cases, three to five conversations are enough.) The five tasks, skillfully employed, are effective, respectful, and oriented toward justice; they focus on identity, agency, and meaning so that couples can name, access, and build on existing gifts, graces, and competencies. This focus leads to conversations that are hopeful and support covenant relationship. Finally, these tasks help position the caregiver as a "useful consultant" rather than as an expert in couples therapy. This stance helps caregivers establish and sustain the psychological, spiritual, and social boundaries necessary to prevent harm in spiritual care and other helping relationships.

Spirit[3] is already present in a couple's life, working for positive change; the task of the empowering caregiver is to help partners identify, discern, and respond to this life-giving presence. The text assumes the caregiver has an existing relationship with the couple, so that alliance building has been accomplished prior to putting this approach into action. The text also assumes the caregiver has the basic relational and listening skills necessary for effective spiritual care. Finally, the book draws on recent understandings of what helps couples; it emphasizes a collaborative, resource-focused approach that engages a couple's shared stories rather than placing emphasis on deficits, pathologies, and dysfunctional relational patterns. This sets it apart from other spiritual-care texts focused on caring for couples and marriages.

AN APPROACH WITH THREE DIMENSIONS

There are three dimensions to this approach. Its focus is *empowering* couples, not solving their problems or providing something they lack. It takes a *narrative* stance, emphasizing the power of shared stories as well as a particular understanding of how people change. It describes *spiritual care* rather than marriage counseling, psychotherapy, or another type of help. Let's look at each dimension in more detail.

Guiding vs. Empowering

"Guiding" is a classic form of spiritual and pastoral care in the church and other spiritual communities. Often concerned with ethical or moral issues, guidance primarily involves helping people make choices about unfamiliar, confusing, or difficult situations (Mitchell 1990), especially issues of meaning and ultimate concern.[4] Guiding care usually proceeds by drawing on a person's own strengths, resources, and values, or by appealing to external authority such as Scripture, community norms, or a particular religious tradition. *Empowering Couples* emphasizes guiding care in the first sense; it helps caregivers draw out a couple's shared values, strengths, resources, and desires for the future. This approach *strengthens* the shared identity of the couple and *supports* partners in resisting forces that cause distress in their relationship. (This is an *eductive* approach; appealing to outside authority would be an *inductive* approach.)

Although guiding care has tended, historically, to focus on a person's self-awareness and personal wholeness, pastoral theologian Sharon G. Thornton argues that *guiding* in the twenty-first century "involves turning our attention outward as well as inward, so we learn to 'wake up' completely" to suffering caused by sociopolitical realities and systemic injustice (2002: 123). She reenvisions guiding care as a communal practice of *empowering for healing*—that is, raising consciousness so that people can "connect personal pain with public tyranny and devise strategies to alleviate both" (ibid., 124). *Empowering* care allows people to claim their agency; it brings them to voice so that they can act rather than be acted upon, and it leads them to act in solidarity with others to end suffering (ibid., 154–63). When *guiding* becomes *empowering*, those who suffer become the primary agents of change; the caregiver is no longer directive, coercive, or positioned "over" or "above" those seeking care.

The "empowering guidance" I advocate can be imagined as a type of conversation rather than as formal counseling. It critically integrates spirituality with empirical data about successful marriages to advocate for mutuality and cooperative partnership within covenant relationships. Caregivers who adopt this approach will tend to "travel lightly" in terms of pastoral and professional power, decentering themselves so that couples can identify and build on their unique strengths, resources, and relationship with Spirit. As such, this empowering guidance is appropriate for the sorts of ordinary conflicts and tensions that emerge between partners. (But be wary: this would not be an appropriate form of care for highly volatile couples or those whose primary struggles relate to violence, addiction, infidelity, or severe mental illness.) My overarching goal with this approach is to allow partners to create a covenant friendship strong enough to resist forces that threaten relationship (sometimes without our awareness), especially the negative influences of criticism, defensiveness, contempt, and withdrawal, which are generated in part by cultural roles and expectations.

Narrative Approaches to Giving Care

People live by the stories they tell—stories about their pasts, presents, and possible futures. These stories include identity, plot, action, time, and agency—all elements of narrative. In fact, narrative is so pervasive in our lives that psychologist Dan P. McAdams has written:

If you want to know me, then you must know my story, for my story defines who I am. And if *I* want to know *myself*, to gain insight into the meaning of my own life, then I, too, must come to know my own story. I must come to see in all its particulars the narrative of the self—the personal myth—that I have tacitly, even unconsciously, composed over the course of my years. It is a story I continue to revise, and to tell myself (and sometimes to others) as I go on living. (1993: 11)

This is just as true for couples as for individuals. Each couple tells at least three stories about the relationship—the story each partner tells individually (for a total of two) and the shared story they tell together. All of these accounts fall somewhere along a "good story/bad story continuum" (Ziegler & Hiller 2001: 3ff.) that sees the relationship as primarily positive or primarily negative. Our task as caregivers is to help the couple move their accounts as close as possible to the positive, "good story" end of things.

Anytime we provide care, we are intervening—intentionally or not—in the stories people tell. We become characters in the narrative of their lives, and we influence the plots and subplots by which they account for what happens in their day-to-day experience. The caring approach in *Empowering Couples* makes intentional, explicit use of the stories that couples tell about their relationships. The goal is to coach them toward telling more helpful and positive stories as they inch toward the "good story" end of the narrative continuum. In the process, we focus on the couple's identity, agency and meaning-making, deconstructing unhelpful cultural accounts of what "normal" partnerships look like (or what they achieve) in order to privilege the couple's own vision of what their partnership can be. At its best, that vision will emerge organically from the values and spiritualities of the partners in covenant through a process of spiritual caregiving and care receiving.

Spiritual Care in Context

Spirit pervades everything—from pumping gas and shopping for laundry soap to eating wonton soup and trimming the rosebushes. We can't escape it. That means all care has a spiritual dimension. But the approach presented here is *spiritual care* for five reasons. First, I assume that readers bring some spiritual or faith commitments to their practices of care. When caregivers have critical and imaginative commitments to a particular spiritual tradition (or traditions), bringing to their care an allegiance to particular sacred texts, values, worldviews, and spiritual practices, their care will be spiritually integrative to some degree. Second, the text requires caregivers to access, implicitly if not explicitly, the values and spiritualities of the couples they work with as one way of empowering partners. Third, my approach adopts and adapts the aims of spiritual care for families proposed by pastoral theologian Herbert Anderson: empowering people to embrace paradox, seek justice, acknowledge finitude, and practice hospitality in the face of fear and contingency (2009: 196). Fourth, I write as a pastoral theologian, spiritually integrative counselor, and Fellow of the American Association of Pastoral Counselors; thus the text stands in the long tradition of pastoral care and counseling literature that has emerged primarily from the North American mainline church and the progressive theological academy.

Finally, spirituality as a whole is an important aspect of a couple's experience together. There is some evidence that spiritual beliefs and practices contribute to healthy family functioning, and many people consider spiritual beliefs and practices essential factors for strengthening families and couples. In addition, couples encounter religious and spiritual issues throughout their life together, from early considerations that surround the making of covenant commitments to questions related to raising children to death rites and rituals. As family therapist Froma Walsh writes:

> From a family systems perspective, there is a mutual influence between spirituality and the family: Meaningful spiritual beliefs and practices can strengthen families and their members; in turn, their shared spiritual experiences strengthen members' faith. Likewise, harsh or oppressive spiritual beliefs and practices can wound family members, their spirits, and their relationships; in turn, those who have been injured often turn away from their faith. (2009: 19)

Some readers might ask, quite rightly, how I am using the term *spirituality* (and its adjectival form *spiritual*) in the text. Definitions of "spirituality" abound, and almost all of them are deficient in one way or another. In this text, the term refers to "both a way of seeing and a pattern for living" (Anderson 2009: 194). That way of seeing and living is individual and communal; teleological; liberating; able to grant security in the midst of anxiety; and has internal and external, active and passive, and deliberative and interpretive dimensions. Spirituality manifests in diverse forms, varying from culture to culture and from person to person across the life span, but it has a consistent and constant goal: "to be open to the transcendent dimension of life present in ordinary, everyday activity" (ibid.). Within this understanding, caregivers might consider couples to be "communal souls" (ibid., 195), a living unity of two human individuals and the divine, a unity that has a wholeness and direction absent from either partner as an individual.

Fam.ly / Couple

FOUR RESOURCES FOR CARE

Woven through the three dimensions of the book—empowerment, narrative, and spiritual care—are four resources: spirituality, psychology, science, and theology. The first resource is an ancient Semitic[5] understanding of "passions"—sometimes called "spirits" or "demons"—found in the early desert traditions of Christian spirituality. Arguments about the existence and nature of spirits and demons as ontological realities are beyond the scope of the text; as I am using these terms, they refer to the "powers and principalities" (Eph. 6:12; Wink 1992) that create strife in committed relationships. I understand the terms as helpful metaphors for understanding and addressing the difficulties that can come between partners; thus I am using them as epistemological rather than ontological placeholders.

Second, I turn to narrative psychotherapy as a consistent and coherent model of change that is appropriate for use with couples. Developed in New Zealand and Australia, narrative psychotherapy is a modality of care increasingly used by spiritual and pastoral caregivers such as Andrew D. Lester (1995), Christie C. Neuger (2001), and John Blevins (2005). Neuger notes that narrative-counseling theory "is efficient, effective, empowering, and deeply relational" (2001: x), based on hope and the idea that "human beings are makers of meaning at their deepest core" (ibid.). She continues:

> Narrative theory's efficient and effective qualities, as well as the de-centering of the counselor in the counseling process, make

this approach well suited to parish pastors. Its respectful and advocative nature makes it well suited to a liberationist theological commitment. Its care for the particular story in the midst of dominant cultural discourses makes it well suited for working with women. Its focus on hope and possibility makes it well suited for all. (Ibid., x–xi)

From my perspective, these same traits make narrative therapy an appropriate approach to spiritual care with couples. In addition, it offers a model of change suitable to brief intervention; much can be accomplished in five to seven conversations when working from a narrative perspective.

Third, the empirical research of psychologist John Gottman (1999) provides a norm for the text. Gottman and his colleagues (first at the University of Washington and now in his own independent laboratory) use scientific data and direct observation to identify what makes a partnership stable and what harms it beyond repair. Through this work, Gottman developed a model that he says can predict with 90 percent accuracy which newlywed couples will remain married and which will divorce within four to six years. An approach to couples therapy developed around Gottman's research seeks to maximize and reinforce the positive, protective factors in couples' interactions and to minimize destructive factors.

This text uses Gottman's understanding of a healthful relationship as a pragmatic norm. It also reimagines what Gottman calls the "Four Horsemen of the Apocalypse"—criticism, defensiveness, contempt, and stonewalling—as dangerous spiritual passions that divide a couple and drive partners apart. Gottman considers these behaviors among the most destructive actions within a partnership, and this text accepts and builds on that scientifically demonstrated conclusion.

Finally, the text assumes a theology of mutuality in which relational justice, mutual empowerment, respect for embodiment, and resistance to colonization by harmful cultural norms are criteria by which a healthful covenant partnership that meets personal and relational needs can be distinguished from a harmful, patriarchal, or hierarchical partnership focused on meeting cultural needs. Healthful partnerships emphasize relational competence rather than role competence, and, in Christian contexts, accept voluntary mutual submission, mutual self-giving, and mutual support, as depicted in Ephesians 5:21-33, as norms for behavior (Taylor 1999: 79). Enemies of healthful partnerships, from the perspective of a theology of mutuality, include economic, social, and cultural forces and the fears, hurts, and distorted visions of the partners (ibid., 80).

OVERVIEW OF THE TEXT

As described above, this text adopts Sharon Thornton's proposal that the classical mode of care as *guidance* be reenvisioned as a practice of *empowering* people to act for justice on their own behalf. As couples make this effort, spiritual caregivers work to sustain them, always looking toward reconciliation through acts of solidarity—acts focused on doing justice. Thus the book has an inherent focus on *liberating justice* as an orienting value for contemporary covenant relationships. This is reflected in the first chapter, "Mutuality and Partnership: Theological Norms," which provides a normative understanding of a healthful and life-giving covenant relationship for the twenty-first century.

Chapter 2 critically correlates Gottman's empirical research on the four most common behaviors that undermine partnership with the destructive spiritual passions emphasized by the early desert tradition of Christianity. The desert tradition's methods of neutralizing the passions—primarily confession and equanimity—are explored as pathways by which couples can minimize the influence of contempt, criticism, defensiveness, and stonewalling.

Chapter 3 introduces a narrative approach to addressing problems between partners, framed through the "SMART" approach to counseling proposed by social-work researcher David Nylund (2000). The chapter places particular attention on the assumptions of the approach and the attitudes that guide its practitioners. By correlating this approach with Gottman's research, the chapter addresses the theospiritual theme of *embodiment* by highlighting the need for caregivers to attend to and diffuse the physical arousal (characterized by the "fight or flight response") that accompanies couple conflicts. The chapter concludes by emphasizing the fit of a modified SMART approach with the text's theological emphasis on mutuality and partnership.

Chapters 4 through 8 lead the reader through each step of the modified SMART approach, illustrating how to implement the approach advocated by the text. Case examples from across the life span of a relationship demonstrate in vivid, concrete ways how caregivers can apply the practical tasks of empowering guidance. A primary goal is for caregivers to understand what specific steps are to be taken and to be able to envision themselves using the approach in their practice of care, be that parish ministry, social work, pastoral counseling, or informal conversation as a volunteer caregiver.

SCOPE AND LIMITATIONS

Like much of my scholarship, this book represents an ongoing effort to catalyze a "turn to wisdom" in the disciplines of pastoral and practical theology. By "turn to wisdom," I mean an intentional and critical choice to elicit, access, and interpret lived spiritualities—historic and contemporary, formal and informal, Christian and non-Christian—and the academic discipline of spirituality as a source, norm, and resource for practices of care and counseling. Because the book emphasizes the correlation of desert spirituality with narrative therapy and empirical research on couples' behavior, I limit engagement with other topics that have been central to pastoral and practical theology for the past twenty years. Chief among these less-acknowledged themes is gender.

Gender dynamics and gender equality are central concerns when caring for couples, especially heterosexual couples. Yet I suspect that feminist and womanist readers will criticize me—rightly and deservedly—for inadequate attention to gender throughout the text. Because a full treatment of gender concerns is beyond the scope of the book (and the series in which it appears), I emphasize only those elements of gender that Gottman's research identifies as behaviorally significant. Likewise, I do not significantly address race, ethnicity, class, or sexual orientation and sexual fluidity as variables that shape the interaction between partners and among couples and their caregivers. There is ample literature available on these subjects for readers who want to know more. I trust that most will accept the book for what it is and forgive its shortcomings.

INFLUENCING THE STORY

What we think and know, of course, is shaped by our communities and experiences. I write as a Presbyterian pastor, a practitioner of Theravada Buddhism, and an educated, white, sexually fluid man and father in a heterosexual marriage for nearly a quarter century. Professionally, I am a pastoral theologian, spiritually integrative counselor, seminary professor, spiritual director, and Minister of Word and Sacrament in the Presbyterian Church (USA). My religious-spiritual identity is Buddhist Christian; my theological orientation is Reformed and liberationist. In keeping with my theological heritage, I consider covenant, joy, God's desire for us and our desire for God, and the public good central to my understanding of covenant partnerships. Sex, procreation, and gender roles rarely influence my theologizing about marriage and covenant partnerships.[6]

ACKNOWLEDGMENTS

Every text is woven from a host of formative conversations, as well as the efforts of invisible colaborers. It is impossible to acknowledge all of them, but some are so primary that they must be named. I am grateful first to Howard Stone, emeritus professor of pastoral theology and pastoral counseling at Brite Divinity School, Texas Christian University, Fort Worth, and editor of the Creative Pastoral Care and Counseling Series, for insisting that I write this text. Likewise, I am grateful for the patience, encouragement, and work of the editorial team at Fortress Press that brought this book to market: my editor and friend David Lott, whose wisdom shines throughout these pages; former managing editor Susan Johnson; and former editor-in-chief Michael West. The trustees, president, and dean of Claremont School of Theology provided a generous research leave, during which I completed the manuscript. Joy Allen, MDiv, LCSW, provided meaningful and helpful feedback on chapter 2. Several research assistants provided assistance: Cathey Edwards at Phillips Theological Seminary; Krista Wuertz, Insuk Kim, Katherine Rand, and Anna Cho at Claremont Lincoln University and Claremont School of Theology; and my personal assistant, Arvind Kumar. Librarians Sandy Shapoval and Clair Powers at Phillips Theological Seminary set a new standard for generosity and patience. Students in Spiritual Care and Counseling for Couples and Families have been inspiring conversation partners at Claremont School of Theology and Claremont Lincoln University. Jim Collie and Tim West provided quiet, hospitable space (and nourshing meals) as deadlines loomed. And, as always, I am grateful to my life partner, Karee Galloway, to whom this book is dedicated. She taught me nearly everything I know in my bones about empowering, long-term, covenant relationship and the importance of covenant friendship.

1

MUTUALITY AND PARTNERSHIP

Theological Norms

While Thom is at work and the children are in school, Donna spends hours alone each day. Yet when Thom returns from his blue-collar job, he is not interested in talking or watching movies together; he prefers to play with the kids until bedtime and then drink beer and listen to music alone. When Donna expresses her loneliness and asks about his distance, he becomes defensive and says, "I'm just tired, Donna! Why are you always focused on yourself? Can't you give me some space?" Thom always apologizes after an outburst like this, but Donna's initial anger has become bitter sadness; she is convinced that she has done something to ruin their relationship.

Malik'a and Alejandro function well as partners and as parents of Alejandro's children from another relationship. But nine months into their marriage they are discovering that the little frictions of living together are creating significant tensions— Malik'a squeezes the toothpaste from the middle, Alejandro uses clean plates from the dishwasher rather than putting them away, and neither is used to sharing space instead of enjoying solitude. To top it off, their extended families are less accepting than expected of their cross-cultural marriage; when the couple was dating, their cultural differences seemed exotic and fun, but now those differences are a source of conflict and protracted negotiations about family expectations. In short, marriage is harder than Malik'a and Alejandro expected, and they are frustrated by the relationship and disappointed in each other and in each other's families. Tensions are growing.

Jay was devastated when he discovered that Lisa and a coworker had an affair while traveling together on a business trip. He forgave her but experiences major anxiety each time she travels for work, which she does nearly two weeks each month. Meanwhile, Lisa has grown distant and self-critical, spiraling into depression that prevents her from keeping up with her household chores or attending to Jay's increasingly desperate sense that their relationship has failed. More and more, he seeks emotional comfort from a single coworker when Lisa is traveling, a fact that Lisa seems to ignore.

Intimate partnerships are at risk around the world. Couples colonized by the logic of the global market (as all of us are, to one degree or another, in this second decade of the twenty-first century) tend to treat relationships as means to happiness rather than as ends in themselves. At the same time, the impersonal forces of modernization and globalization create intense social, political, and economic dynamics that tend to work against couples who work at caring with fidelity for each other and for their families (Browning 2003). Economic instability, heterosexual privilege, cohabitation and other alternatives to marriage, the consumptionist-consumerist values of global capitalism, and the growing influence of critical social theories that unmask power and inequality in relationships are just a few of the forces that create challenges and possibilities for couples. Despite these challenges, however, many people have higher—and more idealistic—expectations for marriage and other partnerships than at any time in history.

Shifting needs are part of the reason. "For longer than not," family therapist David Schnarch (2009, 1997) writes, "marriages were arranged for social, economic, and political reasons. Yet, at no time in history have people expected as much gratification and fulfillment from their relationship" (ibid., xvi) as they do now. As social historian Stephanie Coontz writes:

> Because men and women no longer face the same economic and social compulsions to get or stay married as in the past, it is especially important that men and women now begin their relationship as friends and build on it on the basis of mutual respect. You can no longer force your partner to conform to a predetermined social role or gender stereotype or browbeat someone into staying in an unsatisfying relationship. (2006: 311)

Isolated from extended family and other forms of social support, individuals expect their partners to provide intimate companionship that satisfies all emotional, social, sexual, and spiritual needs (Coontz 2006)—yet marriages (and other intimate partnerships) can rarely meet these expectations, as attested by the highest divorce rates in history. In the United States alone, there is one divorce for every two marriages, and on every continent there is evidence of increased distress among couples, including more frequent violence against intimate partners (Browning 2003). The number of marriages in the United States has declined, especially among the poor and the working class, says University of Texas sociologist Mark Regnerus (2012). "[M]arriage is in retreat," he concludes.

But this sort of social analysis—as compelling as it might be—is insufficient for the work of helping professionals, including spiritual caregivers and religious leaders. It is insufficient in part because it is cold and distant, removed from lived experience; it glosses over the particular struggles and sufferings that intimate partners endure, erasing the people behind the statistics.

The same sort of erasure occurs in a culture of professionalism that privileges diagnosis, intervention, and expert knowledge. Such assumptions tend to frame relational issues as intractable, pathological dilemmas that require the intervention of trained experts to make things better. In the face of such disempowering discourse, couples can feel small, weak, and helpless.

But troubled couples are anything but powerless. They need not wait for professional helpers to rescue them. Most of all, they are more than statistics. Religious leaders, mental-health professionals, spiritual caregivers, and couples workers are all too familiar with the people behind the numbers. When reading the anecdotes that opened this chapter, our culture-bound tendency is to focus on the couples' deficits and perceived pathologies. We overlook their strengths and resources. Thom, for example, is quick to repair his defensive interactions with Donna. Malik'a and Alejandro function in strong, positive ways as parents and in other important dimensions of their partnership. Jay and Lisa manage to maintain their relationship in spite of anxiety and depression, and the decision to forgive Lisa's infidelity has allowed them to remain together despite a major threat to their shared covenant.

This is not sugarcoating the problems these couples face. Those problems are very real. But caregivers must recognize that these couples struggle *and* succeed, have problems *and* have unique strengths—all at the same time. Their struggles and problems do not have to outweigh their successes and strengths; they can learn to use the unique powers of their partnerships to improve their relationships, even without professional intervention.

This book makes the couple relationship—not the individual partners, a religious leader, a spiritual caregiver, or a therapist—the locus of power and change in a troubled partnership. It offers a five-part process by which helping professionals can decenter themselves to become "helpful sidekicks" to heroic couples who are empowered to address their own concerns.

Each chapter describes a part of the approach I am advocating, illustrating it with a particular issue that can insinuate itself between partners, pushing them apart and creating tensions that threaten a relationship. Before describing the approach, however, I need to establish two standing stones as a gateway to a model of care that empowers partners: a *vision* of healthful, mutual partnership that is sufficient for couples navigating the first half of the twenty-first century—that is, a critical utopia of sorts (more on this later)—and a general *account* of what causes distress between partners, what it is that can go wrong in a relationship that requires a focused effort to get things "back on track" and headed in a positive direction for both partners. To that end, this chapter offers a critical theological vision of healthful, mutual partnership; chapter 2 offers an account of what causes distress between partners.

Starting with a normative theological vision is important, theoretically and practically, because spiritual caregivers need—for themselves—a clear and critical place to stand when they care for couples. Some spiritual caregivers (such as chaplains, imams, ministers, rabbis, and others) officially stand between a religious or spiritual tradition, its theology, and a particular partnership in need (Patton & Childs 1988). They listen to both the lived experience of a couple and their own faith tradition, aware that the faith tradition is shaping how they hear the couple. Other spiritual caregivers have a less formal relationship to a particular religious or spiritual tradition but nonetheless have embedded ideas about covenant partnership, ideas shaped by their attitudes toward and experiences with the transcendent dimension of life. Those embedded ideas should be examined and explicitly *chosen* as norms to influence spiritual care, rather than remaining implicit and therefore shaping care without the caregiver's awareness.

Theologies and spiritualities always emerge from particular experiences, values, and commitments, of course. Therefore, the theological norm and vision I advocate here are expressed from a Christian perspective; they are expressed this way because I write as a Christian pastor in the Reformed tradition. My identity leads me to think about marriage and covenant in unique ways. Other Christians will disagree, and people of other religions might find my proposal confusing. I offer this reflection, then, not as a universal theological truth about covenant partnerships, but as one way of thinking about partnership that is congruent with a particular theological and spiritual tradition. I hope it is useful as you think critically, from the perspectives of your own spiritual and religious traditions, values, and commitments, about the theological and spiritual understandings of marriage and other covenant partnerships that inform your approach to empowering couples.

Family is one such partnership

THE FUNCTION OF INTIMATE PARTNERSHIP

For most of the premodern and modern periods of history, patriarchal dominance—male headship, female submission—was the primary form of covenant relationship, including marriage, in the North Atlantic regions. This hierarchal structure remains the dominant form of intimate relationship in many (if not most) regions of the world today. These statements are sweeping generalizations, of course; they do not represent the nuances of particular times and places—early Christian marriage, for example, seems to have been a challenge to the male-dominated households of the Greco-Roman period of the Mediterranean region (see Osiek & Balch 1997). Nonetheless, the pattern of male headship and female submission informs many of the legal, economic, religious, and cultural norms for covenant relationships around the world.

As a result, some contemporary debates about marriage and family tend to be framed in terms of *family structure* and *gender-role competence*. These frames carry two implicit assumptions: first, that covenant partnerships should be structured hierarchically (and usually patriarchally) to promote sociocultural and religious ends; and second, that successful relationships require partners who comply with cultural expectations about gender, power, and relational roles so that the needs of social institutions are fulfilled. These assumptions have shifted in the past fifty years, of course, but they are still deeply embedded in U.S. American subcultures and in broader gender assumptions, as well as actively promoted by some religious, political, and social organizations. They can be one source of tension in contemporary covenant partnerships.

Another source of tension is the shift from sociopolitical and economic reasons for marriage to the primacy of intimacy and love as motivations for joining together. As companionate marriage— that is, partnership established to satisfy relational needs rather than societal requirements—became the contemporary norm, relational competence became more essential than role competence (Taylor 1999: 62–63). Yet many people never learn the relational skills to maintain intimate partnership; they are socialized into role competence. As a result, a couple's energy and attention turn inward as they learn new relational skills to maintain emotional connection. This erodes the role that covenant partnerships once played in the public sphere; their function has become primarily private: serving the intimacy needs of each partner.

In the Christian traditions, however, covenant partnerships have both a communal and private function: the care of generations (Patton & Childs 1988: 12). Helping couples care for themselves, their parents, and their children should outweigh concerns about family form or structure, argue pastoral theologians and marriage-and-family therapists John Patton and Brian H. Childs:

> "What is normative, or essential, for human beings is the care of the generations that immediately touch our lives—usually the generations before, one's own generation, and the generation after. . . . The quality of care for the generations that are closest to us by choice or circumstance is more important for Christian family living than the present form or structure of our households" (ibid., 13).

They base this assertion on the biblical and theological understanding of humans as relational and temporal beings created in the image of God. From this perspective, they state that a marriage (and, I would add, any other covenant partnership) "endures and fulfills its purpose when the human capacity for caring is continually expressed and developed through it" (ibid., 99).

I embrace Patton and Child's proposal that *the care of generations* serves as a functional norm for Christian covenant partnership. It fits a biblical understanding of the human being, positions covenant partnership as vocation, allows for a variety of relational and family forms, and nicely identifies a couple's private and communal obligations. It further emphasizes that ongoing care for the covenant partnership must be prioritized if a couple is to care successfully for the generations before and after. Because of these strengths (and others), the function of *the care of generations*, rather than the form or structure of a partnership, is a primary norm for covenant partnerships in *Empowering Couples*. This book focuses on helping partners learn to care more effectively for their own generation to sustain their care for the generations closest to them.

However, I disagree with Patton and Childs when they suggest that the function of a covenant partnership can be distinguished sharply from its form or structure. Even if partners provide effective care to others, an unjust marriage or covenant partnership should not be commended; to do so would condone injustice and risk its replication in older and younger generations. Rather, the quality of a couple's caring will be determined in part by the nature and form of their relationship—how power is allocated and used, the meanings and values shared by the partners, the quality of the covenant partnership, and so forth. These dimensions of a couple's relationship are embodied through the form and structure of their life together, which exist in a reciprocal relationship with the functional norm of the care of generations.

Therefore, spiritual caregivers need criteria by which to distinguish helpful and healthful covenant partnerships from those that might be harmful and less healthful. A theology of mutuality in covenant partnership can provide key criteria for this purpose.

A VISION FOR COVENANT PARTNERSHIP

Mutuality and partnership are primary qualities of a helpful and healthy covenant relationship, one that is consistent with the values and commitments of the God of the Hebrew Bible, the New Testament, and the Christian traditions. These qualities have been named and valued for centuries in the church's conversations about

marriage, and in the past twenty-five years they have been given
new life by theologians, biblical scholars, and spiritual caregivers
who are working toward more accurate and nuanced understandings of marriage, family, and covenant relationship for Christian
contexts. I call the emerging consensus of these scholars a "theology of mutuality," and I offer it here as an ideal, contemporary
vision for covenant partnership.

As a vision of what is possible, a Christian theology of mutuality stands as a corrective to covenant partnerships in which
patriarchy, hierarchy, and unilateral submission are the implicit (if
not explicit) norms. These harmful beliefs and practices are more
accurately considered sociocultural artifacts than legitimate Christian foundations for covenant partnership, and empirical research
suggests that behaviors associated with these norms contribute to
failed marriages. A theology of mutuality, however, promotes positivity, mutual influence, negotiation, and a sense of "we-ness" in a
relationship—factors that contribute to the longevity and success
of covenant partnerships.

Mutuality as a foundation of covenant partnership has its roots
in the Bible itself. The apostle Paul establishes mutuality as a norm
for Christian marriage in Ephesians 5:21-33, which begins, "Be subject to one another out of reverence for Christ." This passage, central to Christian understandings of marriage and family, has been
used historically to support patriarchy and promote the submission
of women. But contemporary scholars argue that the word usually
translated as "submit" or "subject" carries the connotation of giving oneself to another voluntarily for the purposes of influencing
and meeting the needs of the other (Taylor 1999: 77). "Thus," writes
pastoral theologian Charles W. Taylor, "the passage suggests mutual
self-giving as the Christian guideline for marriage" (ibid.). From his
perspective, "Paul asks each partner to sacrifice equally by devoting
him- or herself to meeting the difficult needs of the other." Thus,
Taylor argues that mutual submission, mutual self-giving, and
mutual support are three practices, or behavioral norms, that allow
a couple to sustain their covenant partnership (ibid., 79).

These practices point toward behaviors a caregiver would
expect to see in a partnership being measured against the broad
criterion of "mutuality." But caregivers find it helpful to have
several specific criteria that, taken together, help assess the ways
in which a covenant partnership manifests particular aspects of

a theology of mutuality. Three characteristics named in recent scholarship, and two that I propose, can serve as criteria for such assessment, helping caregivers distinguish helpful and healthful covenant partnerships from those that might be unhelpful or less than healthful. These characteristics are relational justice (Graham 1992), equal regard (Browning et al. 1997), mutual empowerment (Breazeale 2008), respect for embodiment, and resistance to colonization. I address each in turn.

Relational Justice

Pastoral theologian Larry Kent Graham (1992) makes "relational justice" a central concern for spiritual care, calling caregivers to promote relationships of shared power, shared opportunity, and shared rewards among all people. Such relationships, he argues, are marked by reciprocity and mutuality rather than dominance and subordination. Andrew D. Lester, a pastoral theologian, and Judith L. Lester, a marriage and family therapist, suggest that marriages based on relational justice are characterized by freedom, fairness, mercy, forgiveness, and peace (1998). A covenant relationship that embodies relational justice does not favor one person over another, but functions as a true partnership that equally benefits (and allocates equal responsibilities to) each partner.

Equal Regard

Equal regard describes "a relationship between husband and wife characterized by mutual respect, affection, practical assistance, and justice—a relationship that values and aids the self and other with equal seriousness" (Browning et al. 1997: 2). For scholars in the Family, Religion, and Culture project at the University of Chicago, the equal-regard marriage includes public and private dimensions, and it is ideally supported by a social ecology that protects marriages and families from market forces and other systems that work against equal regard and human flourishing.

In an equal-regard relationship, partners elevate mutuality as a central moral value of their life together:

> Equal regard . . . is a strenuous ethic: one respects the selfhood, the dignity, of the other as seriously as one expects the other to respect or regard one's own selfhood. One also works for the *good*—the welfare—of the other as vigorously as one works for

one's own. But one can expect the reverse as well, that the other works for one's own good. Self and other are taken with equal seriousness in a love ethic of equal regard. This is the meaning of the command, "You shall love your neighbor as yourself" (Matt. 19:19). (Ibid., 153)

Loving the other as oneself, however, is not a solitary, ethical practice. Love as equal regard is an intersubjective activity, something two (or more) people achieve together through ongoing dialogue. It demands close attention to the narrative of each person's life, a concept we will discuss in chapter 3. Thus, "*to love the other as oneself means to regard and empathize with the narrative identity of the other just as one regards and empathizes with one's own*" (ibid., 282; emphasis in original). (Narrativity, as we will see, is central to the process of empowering couples through spiritual care.)

Finally, equal regard has a strong social component; marriages and covenant partnerships are socially interdependent, relying on rich social ecologies to sustain them. Browning and his colleagues argue that the government, the community, the religious congregation, the family, and the individual all have roles to play in ensuring the equality and flourishing of covenant partnerships and their families (ibid., 304).

From my perspective, advocates of equal regard place *eudaemonism*, or human flourishing, at the center of contemporary marriage. Flourishing as a theological concept is a relational dynamic that involves both external conditions and internal attitudes (Browning 2010). Yet the equal-regard movement recognizes that, from the perspectives of most world religious and spiritual traditions, human flourishing is a finite good—a relative means toward a greater end, never an end in itself.

Mutual Empowerment

Seeking to end violence against intimate partners and to redeem couples from constraining gender roles and expectations, theologian Kathlyn A. Breazeale (2008) proposes mutual empowerment as an ideal for Christian marriage. Mutual empowerment, the "creative transformation of the partners and their community toward the greater good" (ibid., 3), occurs through the practice of relational power—that is, the ability to influence and be influenced by one's partner and the capacity to sustain relationship—rather than by imposing one's will on another through dominance, submission, the exercise of individual power, or the allocation of power to one partner or another (ibid., 9–10). "The power to receive influence," Breazeale writes, "is found in one's strength to consider the values and desires of another without losing one's own identity and sense of self; in contrast to passive reception, one is openly active to including the other in one's own world of meaning and priorities" (ibid., 13). Relational power is an active choice. This concept resonates with recent marital research that correlates an ability to receive influence from one's partner with successful marriages (Gottman 1999).

Gender roles and expectations endemic to the male headship-female submission model of marriage, Breazeale argues, give rise to power arrangements that constrain who each partner can become, individually and together, within the relationship they are creating (2008: 15). She seeks instead to make the covenant relationship a "locus of empowerment" (ibid., 10), dismantling hierarchy so that partners can chose whether to manifest the possibilities available to them. Because partners bring unequal gifts and strengths to a relationship, equality is impossible; thus, the goal of mutual empowerment is mutuality or right relationship. Within this framework, sin is understood as a violation of interrelatedness. ____

Respect for Embodiment

Partners informed by a theology of mutuality respect each other's bodies. Violence cannot be an option, and they recognize the body and spirit as an integral whole—the "bodyspirit," as it were—for to disrespect the body disrespects the soul. They know that the body's experience can be trusted as a source of information about self, other, world, and Spirit. Physical intimacy and sexuality—as defined and negotiated by the couple—are dimensions of mutuality, mutual empowerment, and equal regard (Breazeale 2008).

Respect for embodiment includes recognition that mutual empowerment, equal regard, relational justice, and mutuality are not simply ethical values or theological ideals; they are embodied practices, ways of being, that must be enacted wisely throughout daily life—while packing lunches, nurturing the elderly, vacuuming the living room, negotiating carpool duties, and scrubbing toilets. As an incarnational faith, Christianity understands that our deepest convictions and our understandings of the holy are expressed through action, which in turn shapes our convictions and understandings. Our values are expressed through the actions of our body. A disembodied theology of mutuality misses the mark and leads us astray.

Resistance to Colonization

Finally, a covenant partnership informed by a theology of mutuality becomes a site of resistance, in which partners work as a team to keep their psyches (and their relationship) from being colonized by constraining or harmful cultural beliefs. These beliefs usually manifest as social norms and unquestioned expectations about gender, sexuality, violence, relational roles, family dynamics, psychopathology, parent-child relationships, and so on. As an aspect of equal regard, each partner advocates for, supports, and sustains the other's efforts to escape these limiting or distorting discourses; both work to resist the effects of these discourses on the partnership. Mutual empowerment and relational justice entail the couple's active participation in release from cultural constraints that prevent the full expression of the image of God inherent to each person's being. Resisting colonization can also be an aspect of a couple's care of generations, as they support the efforts of other family members to escape the effects of harmful dominant discourses.

LIMITS OF THE VISION

We should not equate a theology of mutuality and its constitutive elements with the goal of spiritual care with couples. Total mutuality and perfect partnerships are beyond our grasp; they are ideals we cannot achieve because of human limitations, systemic evil, distorted visions, and economic, social, and cultural forces (Taylor 1999) that work against mutuality and equal regard. For couples, and for those caring with them, a theology of mutuality functions not as a realistic goal but as a critical utopia (Miguez, Rieger, & Sung 2009); in this role, it serves three ends: (1) it establishes a norm for assessing partnerships; (2) it clarifies criteria that allow us to evaluate the ideas used to support or question a particular relationship; and (3) it orients action and behavior (ibid., 105).

Thus a theology of mutuality creates a horizon of possibility, a transcendent vision of a perfected covenant partnership. This vision cannot be achieved by human effort but represents the way things may be when God's purposes have been achieved. Its transcendence is practical in that it allows us to think concretely about how to intervene with couples toward an existential ideal, while recognizing that the vision cannot be wholly realized in history (ibid., 116). In theoretical and practical ways, then, this vision both orients and limits the care we can provide.

IMPLICATIONS FOR SPIRITUAL CARE
AND COUNSELING

When providers of spiritual care have a clear, critical awareness of their ideas about the purposes of covenant partnership and the qualities of a healthful relationship, they are well positioned to begin empowering couples. Of course, merely being aware of primary theological and spiritual values, commitments, beliefs, and practices cannot be a sufficient foundation for providing spiritual care. But this awareness makes visible the ethical and theospiritual assumptions that caregivers bring to their work. That way they can make sure their practices are consistent with their values, and they can be alert to when their assumptions are different from a couple's assumptions. This reduces the chance that caregivers will unintentionally impose their values on the couples they seek to empower.

But all practices are value-laden, and the practices presented in this book seek to be consistent with a theology of mutuality and partnership that is informed by liberation theologies. The practices here support the premise that there is no normative structure or form for Christian covenant partnerships but, rather, a normative *function*: the care of generations. This function assumes that covenant partnerships have both public and private dimensions; that they are embedded and participate in social ecologies and therefore should not be approached in isolation; and that communities of faith and spiritual practice should actively promote the public-communal dimensions of marriage and other covenant partnerships.

The criteria suggested for helpful, healthful covenant partnerships privilege the values of mutuality, respect, and teamwork (or functioning as "one flesh"). Grounded in biblical, spiritual, and theological principles, these criteria are also consistent with empirical evidence about the qualities of successful marriages. Practical theology considers and incorporates the insights of cognate disciplines, especially the social sciences; this means the proposed theology of mutuality is informed by the interactions, physiologies, and interpretive frameworks of real couples. In this way, the theology of mutuality is an earthy, embodied, realistic theology, one accountable to human experience—not an abstract, theoretical, or impractical set of ideas.

The norms of this earthy, embodied theology suggest that spiritual caregivers need an approach to care that attends carefully to power; emphasizes the agency of partners by privileging their choices and values; strengthens the covenant friendship; respects and accounts for embodiment and the ways in which partners live out their values and choices; and helps couples resist sociocultural norms that impose harmful beliefs, expectations, and practices on their covenant partnerships. The narrative approach suggested in this book is sensitive to all of these concerns.

Before turning to a method of care, however, we need an account of how problems happen in a covenant partnership. This is the focus of chapter 2.

2

DESTRUCTIVE PASSIONS

Clara glowered at her husband, who sat at the opposite end of the sofa in their pastor's office. "Tell me again what I can help you with?" Pastor Nancy asked gently.

"He just ignores me all the time," Clara huffed. "Like this morning at breakfast—he sat there across the table, reading the newspaper, drinking his coffee, and never once spoke to me. I couldn't even see his face. All I could see were the real-estate ads on the back of that darned paper."

"Clara, I don't ignore you *all* the time," Chuck barked. "So I like to read the paper in the morning, and I don't like to talk. I'm not a morning person. Can't you respect that? We've been married for twenty years—I'd think you'd be used to it by now."

Pastor Nancy watched Clara roll her eyes heavenward while the corner of her mouth pulled to the side in a disgusted grimace. "Sure, Chuck—I'm used to it. I've been talking to the dog for years. He pays more attention than you do." Chuck shifted his eyes from Clara to the window beside him, turning his body away from her as he did. Uh oh, thought the pastor. This marriage is in serious trouble.

Nancy sees four particular behaviors at work between Chuck and Clara that point toward the possibility of divorce or separation. But she also knows that these behaviors are manifestations of spiritual passions that the couple can learn to resist and overcome together. She is hopeful because the negative behaviors are not the end of the story. If she helps empower them, this marriage can grow stronger and add to the health and happiness of both partners. Her work is first to help them resist the destructive passions that fuel their disagreements and then to help them create a greater number of more positive interactions in their relationship. She is confident that she can accomplish both.

FOUR DESTRUCTIVE BEHAVIORS

Empirical research by psychologist John M. Gottman (1999) identifies four behaviors that are particularly destructive of partnership: criticism, defensiveness, contempt, and stonewalling. These behaviors are so destructive that he calls them the Four Horsemen of the Apocalypse, after the biblical figures that foreshadow God's final judgment and symbolize conquest, war, famine, and death. Their presence points to serious trouble, and they tend to unfold in order: criticism elicits defensiveness; defensiveness leads the partner who criticizes to show contempt for the defensive partner; and contempt causes the defensive partner to withdraw or turn away, which Gottman calls "stonewalling." By tracking these four behaviors alone, Gottman and his associates can predict divorce with 85 percent accuracy (ibid., 51).

The Four Horsemen were identified through research in which Gottman and his associates visually recorded couples as they talked about their relationships. As the couples spoke, the research team monitored respiration, heart rate, stress hormones, skin perspiration, and other physiological factors. Then they correlated how each partner's body responded to particular conversational topics: nonverbal behaviors like sighs, eye rolling, threatening gestures, and turning away; and listening behaviors like interrupting, defending, escalating, criticizing, blaming, positive feedback, negative feedback, and so forth. Gottman and his team discovered that the Four Horsemen, as listening behaviors and nonverbal behaviors, are more predictive of negative outcomes than many other actions. They upset the couple's balance and make it more difficult to recover the type of positive interactions that lead to greater stability.

Given this background, let's look at the exchange between Clara and Chuck and note where the Four Horsemen appear:

Clara: He just ignores me all the time . . . (*Criticism, distinguished from a complaint by its globalizing nature:* "He just ignores me *all* the time." *This is a verbal behavior.*) Like this morning at breakfast—he sat there across the table, reading the newspaper, drinking his coffee, and never once spoke to me. (*Criticism.*) I couldn't even see his face. (*Criticism.*) All I could see were the real-estate ads on the back of that darned paper.

Chuck: Clara, I don't ignore you *all* the time. (*Defensiveness. The fact that he "barks" this sentence suggests that his physiology has been aroused by the criticism—his heart is beating faster, his breaths are faster and shallower, and stress hormones are flooding his body.*) So I like to read the paper in the morning, and I don't like to talk. I'm not a morning person. (*Defensiveness.*) Can't you respect that? (*Criticism.*) We've been married for twenty years—I'd think you'd be used to it by now. (*Possible contempt expressed as verbal behavior.*)

Clara: (*Rolling her eyes and grimacing*): Sure, Chuck—I'm used to it. I've been talking to the dog for years. He pays more attention than you do. (*Contempt, as indicated by her words and her facial expression—a nonverbal behavior.*)

Chuck: (*Shifting his eyes away and turning his body from her*): Silence. (*Stonewalling, as indicated by his nonverbal body language and his silence, a form of verbal communication.*)

Each of the behaviors that Gottman calls the Four Horsemen has its own characteristics and dynamics within a relationship, and some of these dynamics tend to be—but are not always—gendered in particular ways. Men typically use some behaviors more often than women; women tend to use other behaviors more often than men. We see this clearly in the dialogue above, as Clara opens the conversation with criticism and Chuck closes it with stonewalling.

Viewed through the lens of the Four Horsemen, it's no wonder Pastor Nancy thought this relationship was in trouble!

As interactive behaviors, the Four Horsemen contribute to one component of what Gottman calls the "core triad of balance" in a partnership (1999: 31–86). They also influence the other two components of the triad: perception of one's partner and one's own physiology. Simply put, when we are criticized or defensive (*behavior*), our heart rates and respirations increase (*physiology*), making it more difficult to remain positive or to interact in productive ways (*interpretation*). When we feel contempt for our partners or feel that they are stonewalling us (*behavior*), we are more likely to tell ourselves a negative story about our relationship (*interpretation*) and respond with criticism, defensiveness, or stonewalling (*behavior*), which stimulate physiological arousal that makes it difficult to "stay present" to our partners.

Given the power of the Four Horsemen to knock a couple off balance, it is important that caregivers understand these behaviors and how they tend to manifest in a relationship. We examine each in turn below.

Criticism

Criticism, Gottman writes, "is any statement that implies that there is something globally wrong with one's partner, something that is probably a lasting aspect of the partner's character" (1999: 41–42). A valid complaint like, "You didn't bring in the mail today" becomes criticism when it starts with a phrase like "You never remember to . . ." or "You always forget to . . ." When this happens, a simple observation about behavior becomes personal. It feels bad. Likewise when an element of blame is added to a complaint: "You didn't bring in the mail today. What's wrong with you? Don't you care that I've been waiting for my check for weeks?"

In general, Gottman finds that women turn to criticism when men are unresponsive and tend to use criticism more often than men (1999: 44). The use of criticism can prevent men from accepting influence from their partners—and accepting influence is an important relationship skill, an essential tool in repairing damage caused by the Four Horsemen and other behaviors. A more frequent use of criticism by women might also explain why men can more often be experienced as defensive; they enter the conversation in a one-down position, which stimulates physical arousal and activates the fight-flight-freeze response. If husbands seem angry, frightened, or frozen, it's often because their bodies are telling them that those are appropriate in the face of a perceived attack in the form of criticism. Defense seems a reasonable response.

Defensiveness

Defensiveness, Gottman explains, "is any attempt to defend oneself from a perceived attack" (1999: 44). He says that a common form of defensiveness is *whining* while playing the innocent victim: "What are you picking on me for? I didn't do anything wrong. What about all the good things I do? I never get any appreciation. Poor me. I'm *innocent*" (45). Defensive people rarely take responsibility for the problem, which suggests that the other partner is wholly to blame. A counterattack is also a common defensive response: "Oh yeah? Well, what about when you yelled at my mother? You acted like a playground bully!" That last remark—calling your partner a child-ish bully—quickly moves toward contempt.

Contempt

Contempt, Gottman says, "is any statement or nonverbal behavior that puts oneself on a higher plane than one's partner" (1999: 45). Mocking, eye rolling, sneering, and using a condescending tone of voice can all be expressions of contempt. Anytime you act in a way that puts down your partner or makes yourself look better, you are in danger of showing contempt. Contempt is the most corrosive of the Four Horsemen; it eats away at a partnership the way rust eats away at unpainted iron left out in the rain, stealing its strength and durability. Gottman's research even suggests that people with contemptuous partners tend to become physically ill more often than others (ibid., 46). This places contempt in its own category; it is the best single predictor of divorce in Gottman's research, and he recommends that it be labeled psychological abuse and declared unacceptable (ibid., 47). Often, the only meaningful response to contempt is to turn away in silence—a behavior that itself is the last of the Four Horsemen.

Stonewalling

Withdrawing from interaction is Gottman's definition of stone-walling (1999: 46). Sometimes this means one partner leaves the room. Other times it means a partner physically turns away from the other or simply stops talking. Instead of all of the small behav-iors that signal someone is listening—nodding the head, making eye contact, saying,"uh-huh" and "yes"—stonewallers look away from their partners and toward the floor; they keep their neck stiff and immobile, tightening their chin and jaw to avoid showing emotion; and they rarely make noise (ibid.). Gottman describes this as conveying "the presence of an impassive stone wall" (ibid.).

Men use stonewalling more consistently than women. It's as if their souls and spirits leave the room, even though their inanimate bodies stay behind. Men usually stonewall when their physiology becomes so aroused that they cannot stay engaged productively in the conversation; they withdraw in order to soothe themselves. While this serves a positive function for the man, most women find it quite upsetting—especially when they do not understand why it is happening. When women get upset by stonewalling, their blood pressure, heart rate, breath rate, and stress hormones increase, and they try even harder to engage their partner. Now two components of the core triad of balance—physiology and behavior—are missing, making it very likely that communication will fail even if interpretation is accurate.

But the presence of the Four Horsemen—especially criticism, defensiveness, and stonewalling—is not the kiss of death for a partnership. These behaviors show up in all relationships, even those that are stable and positive over the long term. The difference is in how they are handled. When couples treat the Four Horsemen as destructive passions, countering them with positivity that lowers tension, creates humor, spurs interest, and leads to greater affection, their effects are neutralized. It is important, then, to understand the nature and function of spiritual passions in human life.

PASSIONS IN THE DESERT TRADITION
OF CHRISTIANITY

When we use the word *passion* today, we usually associate it with strong emotions, positive or negative. "It was a crime of passion," we might say, or, "They kissed passionately." Argentineans are passionate people. Dogs bark passionately at the UPS driver. A person might say, "I feel passionately about ending the war," or "Orchids are my passion." But in the desert spirituality of early Christianity, *passion* had little to do with emotion, and it was seldom positive. Instead, the passions were negative attitudes, energies, and powers that caused people to behave in nonvirtuous ways. They were to be avoided, overcome, conquered—not enjoyed or celebrated.

These ideas evolved in the third through sixth centuries among women and men hungry for God; they had left the cities to practice a solitary, contemplative style of Christian spirituality in the deserts of what are now Egypt, Syria, and Palestine. We call these men and women the desert *abbas* and *ammas*, or desert fathers and mothers. Seeking solitude and experience with God away from an emerging church hierarchy in the urban centers (Demacopoulos 2006), the desert mothers and fathers developed sophisticated understandings of how to live and love toward union with God. In this ongoing practice, overcoming the passions was a primary concern as these seekers sought to develop a loving disposition that echoed the image of God in which they were created.

Just what were these "passions" that the desert mothers and fathers fought against? The passions are a "conglomerate of obsessive emotions, attitudes, desires, and ways of acting that . . . blind us in our dealings with ourselves, each other, and the world, and so pervert perfectly good and useful impulses which take away our freedom to love," writes church historian Roberta Bondi (1987: 57). There is no checklist or handbook that defines them; they are not that static, but alive, impish, and limitless. Simply put, the passions can be anything that distorts (Bondi prefers the word *perverts*; 58) our vision and destroys love. A strong emotion, a state of mind, a habit, a way of seeing the world, a cultural belief, fidelity to a role that doesn't fit—anything can become a destructive passion. Things that become passions don't start off badly, and they might not be destructive in particular contexts. But for some reason, in a particular case, they distort our vision and corrode our ability to love.

Passions don't only affect individuals, either. Biblical theologian Walter Wink (1998) calls communal passions the Powers That Be, locating them firmly within the sociospiritual structures of the world. The Powers That Be, he says, are the unique spiritualities of various systems meant to operate for the good of humanity. "They exist in factories, medical centers, airlines, and agribusiness, to be sure, but also in smaller systems such as families, churches, the Boy Scouts, and programs for senior citizens" (1998: 26). If these systems lose sight of their vocations of serving the good— of embodying God's love for the sake of humanity—and instead begin to serve idolatrous ends, they end up dominating people rather than serving them. Sometimes the Powers, like the passions, dominate partners by forcing them apart.

Wink is clear that the Powers That Be—the passions—have no power over us until they are embodied in living systems or groups of people (1998: 26–27). "The issue is not whether we 'believe' in them," he writes,

> but whether we can learn to identify them in our actual, everyday encounters. . . . When a particular Power becomes idolatrous—that is, when it pursues a vocation other than the one for which God created it and makes its own interest the highest good—then that Power becomes demonic. The spiritual task is to unmask this idolatry and recall the Powers to their created purposes in the world. (Ibid., 29)

So how do we identify the passions and Powers in our everyday encounters? One key to identifying a passion is to notice when something works against the common good. In a partnership, this often manifests as something that destroys positive feelings, dispositions, and actions. For example, if one partner says, "Honey, I love you, and I'm sorry I acted that way," and the other responds angrily, "Well, it's about time you apologized!" there is a passion at work. If one partner says, "Silly me—I didn't mean to sound grouchy. Let's try that again," and the other partner remains silent—well, there's a passion at work there, too, in the form of silence. Passions can take almost any form, depending on context. But they always act to cancel out positive intentions, to dilute or destroy love.

They accomplish this by distorting our vision. "The passions blind us so that we cannot see love," Bondi says. "They create for us interior lenses through which we see the world, lenses which we very often do not even know are there. When we are under the control of our passions, even when we think we are most objective, we cannot be—we are in the grip of emotions, states of mind, habits that distort everything we see" (1987: 65). When we cannot see clearly, we cannot act with freedom; the passions have control, and they never choose love.

So it is with Gottman's Four Horsemen. They prevent couples from seeing clearly what is happening in their relationships, and they prevent partners from choosing to act in loving ways. I contend that the Four Horsemen are particular forms of spiritual passions that manifest between partners to keep them from working as a team. Without working as a team, partners cannot address the problems that keep them apart. The nature of this process deserves examination.

HOW SPIRITUAL PASSIONS CAN DESTROY COUPLES

Chuck sat at the coffee shop after the meeting with Clara and the pastor. "Always ignore her?" he muttered to himself. "Never speak to her? Like hell, I don't. She disrespects me all the time, just like she did today. No good for me. And she thinks I pay less attention to her than the dog does? I can make that happen." He paused for a sip of black Colombian. *Always ignore her*, he thought again. *Why did she say that? Am I really that bad a guy? Do I make her that unhappy? Why do I even go with her to talk to the pastor?*

Doesn't do a damned bit of good. He muddled over their conversation for the rest of the day, unable to let go of the criticisms Clara had thrown at him. As soon as he saw her at home, he thought, *Always ignore her, do I?* and called the dog to him instead of greeting Clara.

All couples tell a shared story about their relationship. The "we-ness" (Gottman 1999) of their partnership is vested in this story, which serves as a bond in the covenant friendship.[1] The story contains their hopes, dreams, goals, aspirations, shared symbols, and, often, rituals of connection. The sense of mutuality and positive partnership in a relationship—the prime indicators of health, as discussed in chapter 1—is maintained by this shared story, which ranges along a continuum between the poles of a "good story" and a "bad story" (Ziegler & Hiller 2001). When things are going well, the couple's account of their relationship tends toward the "good story" end of the continuum; when things are not going so well, it tends toward the "bad story" end of things—like Chuck's account at the coffee shop. The story—good or bad—is maintained by each partner's perception of the relationship, and perception is one component, along with physiology and interactive behavior, of the core triad of relational balance posited by Gottman (1999).

The passions work to destabilize this core triad and destroy a sense of mutuality and partnership. They worm their way between partners, creating a fissure in two people's sense of "we-ness" that can then expand until there is a vast gulf between them. The passions first surface as interactive behaviors—the act of criticizing, for example, or of freezing out one's partner with silence—but they soon influence the physiology of each partner, causing heart rates to increase, stress hormones to cascade through the body, and a fight-or-flight reaction to begin. At this point, it becomes impossible to listen to each other. Because of the physiological arousal, the brain's interpretive function is primed to perceive threats and to protect against them. Conversations escalate into arguments; arguments become fights. Nothing positive can survive; only negative energy is possible.

Even one negative interaction primes the pump for more—literally wires the brain to expect (and enter into) negative interactions with your partner in the future. When this happens, the interpretive component of the core triad of balance starts to corrode. Each partner begins to develop negative subplots in the shared story, just like Chuck does over his cup of coffee—subplots about how bad their partner is, about how unhappy they are in the relationship, how seldom their needs are met. Passions feed on this sort of rumination; they grow stronger, and they invite other moods, thoughts, and experiences that hold the potential of becoming passions too.

Men especially are prone to this process (Gottman 1999), replaying interactions in their minds, chewing on small irritations like they were a piece of gristle from a steak, worrying them like a dog with a bone, until they grow into full-blown passions. "It is only when we seize hold of the thought or the image or the mood, brooding on it and feeding it and encouraging it to grow, that we become responsible," Bondi writes. "This is the point where it starts to become a passion. Though a full-blown passion seems to have a life of its own while we are held helpless in its grip, the contention is that passions do not start with this kind of power over us" (1987: 69).

But once a passion does have that power, and if the process described above is not reversed, the shared story can gradually become two negative stories about the relationship, and then the shared story becomes a distant memory. The more distance the passions manage to put between partners, the more difficult it is for a couple to work as a team to revive a positive shared story and reestablish their covenant friendship.

This progression is rarely as linear as I've suggested, of course. Instead, it occurs in fits and starts; partners move apart, then come closer together, then move further apart as the passions continue to gnaw at the core triad of balance, working to create distance. Couples with a strong, positive covenant friendship find it easier to resist the passions, so the destruction of the partnership occurs slowly, if at all; couples whose covenant friendship contains more negativity from the beginning find that the passions establish a presence faster and create distance more rapidly. And the presence of the passions doesn't necessarily mean a relationship will inevitably dissolve; it simply means the couple needs to act as a team to neutralize or resist the passions as quickly as possible. Both Gottman's research and the desert mothers and fathers suggest ways of calming the passions and working to expel them from a person's life. Poor Chuck could stand to hear about them!

RESISTING THE PASSIONS

For Gottman (1999), the way to neutralize the Four Horsemen is to enhance the marital friendship, particularly by increasing the fondness and admiration that partners express toward each other; increasing the emotional bank account so that partners are more likely to turn toward each in ways that reflect emotional connection rather than distance; and increasing the number of positive interactions between partners. (His research shows that couples in happy, stable marriages have five positive exchanges for every negative interaction; 35.) The tradition of desert spirituality relies on at least three spiritual practices to resist and eradicate the passions: introspection, confession, and equanimity. Let's look at each one.

Introspection

Introspection literally means "looking within." As used by the desert mothers and fathers, it carries the sense of *seeing clearly* and *honestly* who we are—identifying the best parts of ourselves and honestly naming the worst parts. "Introspection means looking inside ourselves to see what it is that makes us tick or fails to make us tick in order that we may love," Bondi writes. "It has to do with observing ourselves to see what we think or feel or do that hurts us or makes us hurt others *so that we can do something about what needs to be corrected, and strengthen what needs to be strengthened*" (1987: 78). In particular, introspection requires us to be honest about the passions—anger, fear, boredom, jealousy, sadness, joy—that prevent us from thinking, speaking, and acting with love. The purpose of introspection is increasing our freedom to choose actions that are consistent with the health of our relationships rather than ones that protect or enhance ourselves at the cost of other people (see Bidwell 2004a). Two methods of introspection are, first, disclosing thoughts—particularly passions—to a spiritual director or trusted friend and, second, seeking feedback from others about habitual ways of being and thinking that might give hints about inner dispositions.

Confession

In the sense it is used here, confession can be understood as the "manifestation" or "disclosure" of thoughts, as discussed in relation to introspection. In the disclosure of thoughts, people reveal the thoughts (and the behaviors that resulted from those thoughts) that led to distance between their partners and themselves. It is important that confession not happen defensively; the person confessing needs to be able to look at themselves clearly and honestly in order to be accountable (and forgiven) for their role in allowing passions to create distance in the relationship. Quaker theologian Richard Foster (1988) suggests one way of confessing that can be adapted for use with couples. First, a person or couple and a trusting friend pray together, inviting Spirit to reveal anything in their lives for which they need forgiveness or healing (or both). After a period of silence, the person or friend names aloud those things that Spirit has helped to reveal. Once the confession has been made, everyone sits in silence; the trusted friend ends the silence with words of assurance that the person or couple is forgiven by God. Then the friend prays, giving thanks for God's grace and asking for continued healing and wholeness in the couple's life (ibid., 149–56).

Equanimity

Equanimity literally means "balanced spirit" or "balanced state of being." Spiritual teachers Frederic and Mary Ann Brussat (2010) describe it as "being like the mountain"—stable and solid no matter what weather occurs—rain, snow, or sunshine. In the early Christian traditions, equanimity was a foundation for gentleness, contentment, self-restraint, and charity as a form of love—all qualities that one might find in a mutual and positive partnership. People who have equanimity feel deeply, but they are not knocked off center by their likes and dislikes, desires or aversions. As a consequence, the passions cannot get a foothold in such people; they are too even-tempered to allow the passions to turn them away from their partners.

Such persons have no need to control what happens to them; they feel deeply but do not interfere with what is happening. Criticism and contempt do not elicit negative responses; they do not defend themselves or stonewall, because their inner balance has not been swayed. It's as if they are continuously saying to themselves, "This, too, shall pass." The equanimity of just one partner might well be the strongest defense against the passions in a covenant partnership.

IMPLICATIONS FOR SHORT-TERM SPIRITUAL CARE AND COUNSELING

An understanding of the passions in general and the Four Horsemen in particular can help caregivers understand what causes suffering among couples. Yet, from my perspective, neither Gottman nor the desert tradition offers a sufficient antidote to the passions when it comes to working with troubled couples. The desert practices of equanimity, confession, and introspection are helpful to a certain extent, especially in their attention to the spiritual dynamics that allow the passions to create distance between partners, but the desert tradition is limited in two ways. First, it is too individualistic, focused primarily on the intrapsychic and psychospiritual processes of one partner, and therefore unable to address the relational dimensions of a couple's difficulties. Second, it cannot take into account what we know from science about healthy couple relationships or from psychotherapy about processes of effective change in couple relationships. It can be an adjunct to effective spiritual care for couples, but it is not sufficient in and of itself.

Gottman's approach to resisting the Four Horsemen has strengths, rooted as it is in scientific evidence and relational theory. Yet, what it contributes in terms of empirical validity, it lacks in terms of practical application. Gottman does not provide a clear enough model of change to be helpful to caregivers with limited experience, and his approach is difficult to implement successfully in just a few sessions.

Finally, neither Gottman nor the desert fathers and mothers adequately address the narrative nature of human experience; they do not offer effective methods of intervening in and addressing a couple's shared story in ways that are collaborative, empowering, and unlikely to do harm.

What we caregivers need, then, is a way of addressing the passions that allows us to "walk lightly" alongside a couple as the partners work together to revive a shared story of being teammates in the face of adversity. I believe the practices of narrative psychotherapy offer precisely such a pathway and theory of change. We will explore that in the next chapter.

3

A "SMART" APPROACH TO COUPLES CARE

Pastor Nancy sighed. Her second conversation with Clara and Chuck had gone in circles, rehashing that morning's breakfast interaction—who said what and who didn't speak—over and over. It had ended just like their first appointment: Chuck barely responding, Clara in bitter tears and appealing to Nancy to "fix" Chuck. They left her office in silence. Nancy felt helpless and less than helpful.

"This just isn't working." She sighed as she watched them drive out of the parking lot. "I need some different tools. What do I do with them next week?"

Nancy needs three things: a theory of change appropriate to short-term spiritual care, a counseling method that offers clear steps toward the changes Chuck and Clara want for their relationship, and a counseling theory equal to the spiritual passions and sociocultural hurdles faced by covenant partnerships. A narrative approach can offer all three.

WHAT IS A NARRATIVE APPROACH?

A narrative approach to spiritual care draws on narrative psychotherapy,[1] a helping model developed in Australia and New Zealand during the mid-1980s and early 1990s. Narrative therapists believe we shape our lives and give them meaning through the stories we tell, as well as the stories that are told about us by larger sociopolitical and cultural systems—the Powers That Be, to use Wink's (1992) language. An endless number of stories can be told about any life, depending on the perspective from which that life is narrated. Often, people narrate themselves from the perspective of the dominant culture—the one that tells them that they are "depressed," for example, or "voiceless" or "unimportant" or "powerful" or "privileged." The same culture often sets the standard for what it means to be a "man," "woman," "parent," "lover," "spouse," and so forth.

As psychotherapist Stephen Madigan notes:

> The complexity of life, and how lives are lived, is mediated through the expression of the stories we tell. Stories are shaped by the surrounding dominant cultural context; some stories emerge as the long-standing reputations we live through, and other (often more preferred) stories of who we are (and might possibly become) can sometimes be restrained and pushed back to the margins of our remembered experiences. . . . But whatever the stories are that we tell (and don't tell), they are performed, live through us, and have abilities to both restrain and liberate our lives. (2011: 29–30)

This is where problems come from—the ways in which the stories we tell and don't tell restrain and oppress our lives.

Here's how it works. The dominant culture—the larger stories being told by society, our families, schools, workplaces, and other systems in which we are embedded—decides who and what is "normal." These prevailing ideologies become cultural and sociopolitical stories that shape people's lives. They come to seem "natural"; they are unquestioned; they are just the way things are. It's not that some powerful apparatus forces these larger stories on people; it's that people begin to live as if those stories are true—that is, perform and reinforce them—in their own lives. We actually believe that those stories tell the whole truth about who we are. But narrative therapists are "acutely aware that problems are created in social, cultural, and political contexts . . . that often serve to obstruct and marginalize the very lives of those whom therapists purport to treat" (Madigan 2011: xii). There are other stories that can be told, stories that contradict accounts that see a particular person as a problem, as abnormal, as somehow broken, or "less than."

In Pastor Nancy's conversation with Chuck and Clara, for example, it is clear that Clara believes that Chuck "never" talks to her. It's equally clear that she believes that spouses should talk to each other at the breakfast table. She has storied Chuck as a deficient spouse, and her way of talking about the problem reflects the fact that feelings and experiences are always lived out of the primary story being told; what we select as meaningful is what is given expression. Wouldn't it be interesting to know where Clara got the idea that spouses should always speak to each other at breakfast? What might happen if we looked for other accounts of what kept Chuck from speaking that morning? How would the story change if we examined Chuck's stories about intimate relationships, which might tell him that silence between partners is a sign of deep comfort with one another? It is the meaning behind the behaviors, or, as Gottman (1999) might say, the perception of what is happening, that is important—the values, the hopes, the dreams represented by a husband who does or does not speak over coffee and toast in the morning—rather than the behavior of speaking or not speaking.

Fortunately, a narrative approach provides a map for caregivers that guides their efforts to help people understand and reauthor their stories so that new and preferred meanings can emerge. In the process, people transform problems into more satisfying accounts of their lives.

A "SMART" APPROACH TO CHANGE

The acronym SMART—developed by social worker David Nylund (2000)—describes a five-step, narrative approach to helping children diagnosed with attention-deficit/hyperactive disorder (ibid., 49). Keeping this basic approach, I have modified Nylund's steps to be appropriate for spiritual care with couples. The five steps are:

Separating people from problems and passions. Wise caregivers engage couples in "externalizing conversations." That is, they separate the presenting problem from the relationship and from each partner. This allows the couple to give the problem a name that seems appropriate. Clara and Chuck, for example, might choose Morning Silence as a name for the particular passion that is threatening their relationship. This externalization has the effect of shifting the couple's attention from perceiving the problem as inside Chuck—or in Chuck's behavior—to understanding it as something coming from outside the couple, where they can face it together, less defensively.

Mapping influences. Once the problem has a name and the couple experiences it as external to themselves, the caregiver begins to map influence—first, the influence of the problem on the couple and then the influence of the couple on the problem. This allows the couple to see clearly the ways in which the problem—the passion or passions that have been creating distance between them—affects each of them, what it has cost in terms of their relational harmony, how it works to keep them from aligning as a team. It also allows the couple to identify ways in which they have some influence over the dividing passion(s), maintaining positivity, preventing the problem from taking over completely, standing up to it when its demands become too great. Chuck, for example, might learn that Morning Silence causes Clara to believe that she no longer matters to Chuck; Clara might discover that she can invite Morning Silence to leave by not bringing the newspaper to the table before Chuck arrives.

Attending to teamwork. The caregiver listens carefully for hints of untold stories about times when the couple is relatively free of the problem (or the passions). In particular, the caregiver asks questions and listens in ways that bring forth accounts of teamwork between the partners—overlooked evidence of times when they worked together to overcome the problem or to neutralize the passions. These accounts become the basis for a new story in which the problem is no longer dominant. Pastor Nancy might find out that Morning Silence is only present on weekday mornings—it never shows up on Saturdays or Sundays because Clara and Chuck work together to keep it at bay through a different morning routine on the weekends.

Reclaiming partnership. Alternatives to the problem story become gateways to a new story about positive partnership, in which the couple works mutually as a team to resist the passions and overcome the dominant, problem-saturated story. The caregiver asks questions to enrich the new story of partnership, helping the couple incarnate the hopes, dreams, values, and beliefs that inform it. Further questions help the couple reclaim the partnership that has always existed alongside and at the margins of the problematic story. Enhancing the covenant friendship, as discussed in chapter 2, becomes a central focus of this step of the change process. Chuck and Clara decide, for example, that they want to invite their "weekend selves" to breakfast during the week and plan together ways to make that happen.

Telling the new story. In the final step, caregivers invite the couple to identify and recruit audiences for the new story of mutuality and positive partnership. The audiences help validate and celebrate the new story, providing new locations for its performance and helping to embed its reality in the life of the couple and their community. Clara and Chuck might share with their best friends or with their grown children how their morning routine has changed and what it means to them to bring their weekend selves to the breakfast table Monday through Friday.

These steps toward change, of course, reflect a number of assumptions about the nature of people and how they experience reality. Making these assumptions clear can help caregivers use the SMART steps successfully. The traditions of brief psychotherapy and short-term pastoral counseling also provide useful assumptions for caregivers who seek to empower couples. I highlight eight of these assumptions below and then describe four caregiver attitudes that support and reflect them.

SOME KEY ASSUMPTIONS

Eight key assumptions are important to empowering couples through the SMART approach. You might be tempted to scan this information (or to skip it altogether) because of its "theoretical" nature, but I encourage a close reading. Narrative approaches to giving care are more a philosophy than a set of techniques, and the ideas presented here challenge some foundational assumptions of dominant North American cultures. These assumptions are also quite different from the psychological ideas that shape the ways in which the industrialized West approaches care giving. Although these assumptions are at odds with the dominant culture (as spiritual traditions often are, as well), they generally fit well with some religious wisdom about human beings and about the ways Spirit relates to the created order.

Overall, a narrative approach to empowering couples through spiritual care makes the following assumptions:

1. *Storytelling rights belong to the couple.* Identity is textual, constructed through the stories we tell and the stories that are told about us. Too often, people adapt themselves so well to the normative story of the dominant culture, reproducing it in their own lives, that they do not realize what other tales they might tell about who they are or what their lives mean. They are living a story being told by someone (or something) else. Therefore, an important assumption is that the couple retains the right to tell their own story—the caregiver should follow, not lead, the content of the story being constructed through the helping conversation.

This is an important way of enhancing a couple's agency, especially in view of power issues and structured inequalities. Honoring the storytelling rights of women may be especially important; pastoral counselor Christie C. Neuger (2001) says that the first stage of narrative work with women is that of "coming to voice," being able to tell their own story in their own words—including giving their own name to the problems that oppress them.

Preserving the couple's naming rights seems to fit the processes of introspection and confession in the desert tradition. Words—especially names—have power in many spiritual traditions; being able to name the demon or power that blocks one's freedom gives a person some control over it. The concepts of agency, freedom, and self-determination are also important to many religious communities and ethical systems.

2. *Alternative wisdom resides at the margins.* At the edges of any story—around corners, underneath thin-but-all-encompassing plots, behind totalizing descriptions such as "lazy, disrespectful woman"—are things that people know but might not have noticed. These understandings are rendered almost invisible by the glitz and glare of dominant stories. Postmodern philosopher Michel Foucault called them "local knowledges" (Madigan 2011: 45), alternative wisdoms that can call dominant stories into question but are silenced or unnoticed because of the power and volume of those dominant stories.

Narrative caregivers assume that couples have local knowledge or local wisdom about overcoming passions, problems, and the Powers That Be. They also assume that careful, curious questioning can bring that wisdom to the fore, where it can challenge or deconstruct problematic stories. In the context of working with women, Neuger calls this "gaining clarity"—helping people not only see how dominant stories have influenced them but also to understand where those stories have come from and how they themselves have participated in keeping them alive, even though those stories are harmful to themselves.

Identifying local wisdom and gaining clarity about dominant stories means that individuals and couples are uniquely placed to challenge and undermine the harm being caused by unhelpful stories. "In challenging the dispositions and habits of life that are fashioned by modern power," Madigan writes, "people can play a part in denying this power its conditions of possibility" (2011: 49).

One way of identifying local wisdom is to explore exceptions to the difficulties that couples face. Hidden wisdom often lurks unseen in these problem-free spaces.

√3. *Exceptions to difficulties always exist.* Exceptions, or times when difficulties are absent or less troubling, always exist. Narrative caregivers call them "unique outcomes" or "sparkling moments." The trick is to identify those exceptions, make sure they are significant to the couple, and then amplify and expand the exceptions into a new plotline that creates the possibility of a different experience of life, one free of (or less influenced by) a particular problem or difficulty. From this perspective, change is inescapable and always brings a chance to make life better. Problems or difficulties are temporary; they exist only because of the power we give them by naming them (and focusing on them) as problems. A narrative spiritual caregiver assumes Spirit is always working to make life more abundant for all people; the task of the caregiver and couple is to collaborate with what God is doing to make a particular difficulty a thing of the past.

In some ways, this assumption reflects the discipline that Brother Lawrence, a seventeenth-century Christian monk, called the "practice of the presence of God." From this perspective, God is always present in our lives, a reality as near as our next breath. We must train ourselves, however, to be aware of God's presence that supports and sustains all of creation, always at work repairing the torn strands of the web of being. Identifying and building on exceptions to our difficulties is one way of identifying and responding to Spirit's presence in our lives.

4. *Re-storying is an act of resistance.* The process of identifying and telling a preferred story about their life together allows couples to resist the influence of the particular passions or powers that have worked to separate them. At a sociopolitical level, re-storying can empower couples to resist cultural and systemic accounts of "who they have been, who they presently are, and who they might become" (Madigan 2011: 22) in order to choose different accounts of their life together. In particular, re-storying a preferred, shared story allows couples to begin eliminating the distance that kept them apart for so long, reestablishing the teamwork that existed—to some degree, at least—when they first came together. Neuger calls this stage of narrative psychotherapy "making choices"—that is, choosing what elements to include in a new, preferred story and

what elements of the other, power-laden and problem-saturated story to reject. In many ways, this process reflects the Christian concept of "turning" from one way of life to another—the literal meaning of repentance. Performing the new story in front of a couple's friends and family members, helping to make it real and to function as a new norm in their life, is a stage that Neuger calls "staying connected." All stories are maintained through a web of interconnected relationships that tell, retell, feed, and sustain them.

5. *Avoid diagnostic labels and pathologies.* Because the problem, not the person, is the problem, narrative caregivers avoid diagnostic labels and pathologizing stories. That means a problem or difficulty faced by a couple is not seen as a fault or weakness located within the "family system" or one of the partners, but is viewed as something oppressing the couple from outside. A caregiver working from this assumption seeks to free people from those things that keep them separate from Spirit and from each other. For example, imagine that one partner says, "I'm too depressed to be a good parent." Rather than saying, "What's going on inside that keeps you from being a good parent?" a caregiver working from a narrative approach might respond, "How does the depression keep you from parenting as well as you'd like? Are there times you can stand up to or 'parent through' the depression? Where did your understanding of 'good parenting' come from, and what's its relationship to depression?"

The difference is subtle but important. This commitment to avoiding diagnostic labels and pathologies is consistent with classical spiritual traditions. The desert mothers and fathers who pioneered Christian spiritual guidance were less likely to label a person as "lazy" or "distracted in prayer" than to explore how a negative spirit was distracting the person from God or convincing the person to spend time in activities other than prayer. Beneath this assumption is a conviction that God empowers people to stand up to those things that turn them away from Spirit. God is at work to set people free from those things that oppress them.

This perspective also assumes that human nature is basically good. We are naturally oriented toward God and made in the image and likeness of God, but powers and passions at work in the world thwart our natural tendencies. Sinfulness is understood less as a problem of will or as an inner state than as a temptation or net that snares people from outside. Deadly thoughts and behaviors attack us, luring us away from our original nature as the image of God.

6. *Negotiate rather than impose a caregiving process.* Through a narrative approach to empowering couples, the caregiver and the partners "cocreate" a new reality together. They share power in a mutual, collaborative relationship that respects the self-determinacy of the couple seeking help. That means caregivers try to avoid assuming that they know the goal of care or *the* solution to a couple's difficulty. Rather, they negotiate goals and solutions together with the couple. They seek to empower the couple to help themselves rather than to rely on a professional caregiver.

Behind this assumption is an expectation that human relationships should be mutual and empowering, based on consensus rather than on an imbalance of power. Narrative approaches to giving care emphasize that people need to feel heard and validated and that the process of receiving care needs to enhance people's sense of agency rather than requiring submissive attitudes or coercing them into particular ways of responding or relating.

7. *Focus on the present and future.* In narrative approaches to spiritual care, the past tends to be secondary to the present and future. Caregivers working from a narrative approach do not assume, as do many psychological approaches, that past experiences create the difficulties people face in the present. Rather, they believe that placing too much emphasis on the past can impede growth and change. Looking to the future is the key to nurturing hope for a different life.

Likewise, spirituality affirms that the present is the best guide to understanding how Spirit is active in a person's life and what ways God might be calling the person to be faithful to the future. An emphasis on the present and future keeps a couple focused on an appropriate response to Spirit's action in their lives *now*. This focus is consistent with the emphasis of the desert mothers and fathers, who used everyday, common activities—eating and sleeping, working and playing—as the starting point for spiritual guidance.

8. *Tailor care to the couple.* Narrative spiritual care is not a one-size-fits-all, cookie-cutter approach. Because couples are the experts about their own lives, narrative caregivers pay close attention to the needs and meanings of the people seeking care, shaping the process to a couple's particular circumstances. This approach respects the diversity of human beings.

Similarly, narrative approaches recognize there is no "proto-col" or universal process that serves all couples equally well. The caregiver must listen closely to the couple, adjusting questions and interventions to accommodate the particularities of the partners and their unique relationship. Likewise, the SMART steps do not unfold in a rigid, linear progression, but circle around each other in a helical fashion, repeating themselves with critical differences over time as preferred stories are identified, authored, reauthored, nuanced, and performed until the distance between a couple dis-solves and teamwork is reestablished.

These assumptions translate into four qualities or attitudes that the caregiver embodies during spiritual-care conversations.

ATTITUDES THAT INFORM THE CAREGIVER

Caregivers guided by these assumptions adopt four attitudes that shape the way they interact with couples. These SMART attitudes set the stage for empowering care; the more they are present, in my experience, the more empowering care will be. Nylund, in fact, identifies the first three of these attitudes as "ethical postures" (2000: 51), suggesting that they are less attitudes than principles that embody the good. He argues that they help caregivers make good use of the SMART steps. "These attitudes help them ask the kinds of questions that create possibilities and open space for new stories," he writes (ibid.).

The three attitudes identified by Nylund are curiosity, respect, and hope. To these, I add detachment as a spiritual virtue present in Buddhism, Christianity, Islam, and other religious traditions.

Curiosity

Traditional psychotherapies teach practitioners to be certain of their expertise and authority in treating the problems that people present to them. They tend to tell stories about their patients from within a medical framework, which gives them the power to diag-nose "problems" and then dictate "best practices" to address the diagnosis, often without taking into account the particularities of the person sitting in front of them—or the fact that the "problem" has been created in a certain way through the act of diagnosis.

Caregivers taking a narrative approach, on the other hand, privilege the expertise and authority of the couple seeking guidance.

These caregivers are inquisitive, intensely curious, and never certain that they have understood fully what is being said. They ask question after question—questions they couldn't possibly know the answers to already—to elicit rich accounts of the stories the couple is telling. They are able to live in the ambiguity of not being certain, of not understanding, not knowing (see Bidwell 2004a), and always being on the way to understanding.

Respect

The local wisdom that has been silenced, subjugated, pushed to the margin, and rendered invisible by problematic dominant stories contains great riches. New lives are possible because of the narrative, social, and cultural capital it contains. Narrative caregivers understand and respect this. They show great patience in luring, coaxing, and co-constructing these marginalized local knowledges into the light of day, where they can be developed into preferred narratives if the couple desires. In the process, narrative caregivers are collaborative, always deferring to the preferences of the couple they are empowering, never assuming that the caregiver knows best. They are also vigilant against any bias they bring to the process. They respect the agency and self-determination of the couple at all times—even when that means not exploring or developing local wisdom that the caregiver thinks might be useful or helpful.

Hope

The only bias that narrative caregivers persistently introduce into empowering conversations, Nylund writes, is hope or "tempered optimism" (2000: 52). They continually communicate to couples through verbal and nonverbal means the conviction that the partners, individually and together, have the skills and resources necessary to overcome the passions that are pushing them apart. This hopeful conviction grows from the caregiver's certainty that the textual nature of identity and meaning will yield subjugated wisdom and subplots that allow partners to resist the passions and powers that are creating difficulties. A narrative caregiver believes in a future free of the problem, a new story in which the couple works as a team to resist and conquer the passions that divide. This calm, consistent attitude can empower couples to think and feel the same way about their futures.

Detachment

Caregivers taking a narrative approach are detached from the outcomes of their conversations with couples. After talking about curiosity, respect, and hope, this might seem a paradoxical statement. But I am not talking about detachment as disengagement or lack of compassion and care; rather, I am using the term to signal an attitude similar to the virtue of equanimity described in chapter 2. Detached caregivers do not have a vested interest in the outcome of empowering conversations; they are not attached to a particular story that a couple "should" or "ought" to tell themselves. In fact, detached caregivers confront vested interests and selfish motives in themselves in order to create space to listen to Spirit's leading. Being detached from outcomes is an act of spiritual freedom.

Being attached to a particular outcome or story line can lead caregivers to evaluate one story as superior or inferior to another—placing a limit or bond on their minds, shutting out curiosity and respect. In this state of mind, caregivers begin to advocate for a particular story; this subtly begins to subjugate other possibilities. They cease to ask curious questions; instead, they ask leading questions that they already (think they) know the answers to. They try to sway the couple's attention in a particular direction. They stop discerning what the couple's preferred futures are and begin to recruit them into their own story for who the couple should be and what the couple's relationship should mean. This sets caregivers up for disagreements with the couple—often unvoiced, but disempowering nonetheless.

Narrative caregivers must turn themselves over to the process of constructing whatever alternative stories the couple values. They cannot be invested or attached to particular alternative stories as "best" or "right" or "more adequate" for those with whom they care.

A "SMART" APPROACH IN HOLISTIC PERSPECTIVE

Humans are holistic beings, made up of bodies, senses, emotions, thoughts, and consciousness. Taken together, these dimensions constitute the soul—that unity of being signified by the Hebrew word *nephesh*, the Greek *psyche*, and the Arabic *nafs*. The practice of soul care, then, is literally the care of the whole person—what Christians traditionally call body, mind, and spirit. These dimensions of the person interact and influence each other, as noted in chapter 2.

The state of your body, for example, shapes the way you behave and interpret events; if you are extremely stressed, your behavior will show it, and you will tend to interpret things as a threat. The way you interpret a partner's words and actions influences the body; if you interpret your partner's statement and tone of voice as a threat, your heart rate and respirations are likely to increase. The way you act in response will influence the way your partner interprets what you are saying and what happens in your partner's body.

One of the strengths of Gottman's (1999) model of marital therapy is that it accounts for this totality of the couple as human beings by attending to physiology, interactive behavior, and perception. In fact, Gottman's research suggests that the body is one of the most important dimensions of a couple's interactions; the frequency with which *diffuse physiological arousal* (DPA)—the body's general alarm system—becomes and remains activated is one of the most reliable factors in predicting whether a couple will stay together.

In DPA, many bodily systems are activated at once so that the body can be safe in physical emergencies or cope with situations perceived to be dangerous. The heart speeds up; blood stops flowing to certain organs and to the periphery of the body; blood pressure rises; glucose, a fuel for the body, floods the bloodstream; and fight, flight, or freeze reactions become more likely. "The attentional system becomes a vigilance system," Gottman writes, "detecting only cues of danger, and at this point is severely limited in its ability to process other information" (1999: 75).

This state of arousal is extremely helpful during a car accident or a mugging. It is not so helpful during an argument with your partner. But it is precisely what can happen during an argument. In fact, Gottman says that "(m)arital conflict appears to be ideally suited for generating this kind of diffuse physiological arousal" (1999: 76). When DPA occurs during an argument, the behavioral and interpretive effects can be devastating. It is harder to process information and learn new things, and easier to fall into old habits and old ways of thinking. Men are especially prone to DPA, and their recovery takes longer than women's. Gottman's conclusion is that the best approach to couples therapy is a "gentleness model" (ibid., 85) that promotes the soothing of behavior, perception, and physiology.

This is where a narrative approach to empowering couples becomes helpful. Time and again, I have watched externalizing conversations, curious and off-the-wall questions, the caregiver's respectful and hopeful attitude, and a detached stance toward outcomes diffuse low-level physiological arousal. A SMART approach interrupts habitual, problematic exchanges that would usually lead to DPA. Externalizing, in particular, is helpful because it locates the problem outside of the partners, often eliminating the defensiveness and blame that trigger physiological arousal. When a body does not receive negative stimulation, it will not erupt into DPA. This is one strength of a narrative approach: it helps protect against diffuse physiological arousal. By working directly, in unexpected ways, on the perceptive dimension of the three elements of relational balance, a SMART approach has tremendous effects on the physiological and behavioral dimensions as well.

MUTUALITY, PARTNERSHIP, AND A NARRATIVE APPROACH

By now, I hope it is clear that a narrative approach to spiritual care can provide a model for couples of a way to talk together that is mutual, collaborative, and resistant to both the Powers That Be and the passions that create difficulties for covenant partnerships. In addition, it fosters mutuality by leveling the playing field between partners, placing the problem outside of them and allowing them to become allies in a team against it rather than criticize, defend against, and confront each other over perceived insults and injuries. In this way, partners learn to share relational power, to influence and receive influence from each other, and to build a positive partnership in which both contribute to the emerging story of a problem-free (or problem-resistant)[2] life.

The SMART steps allow caregivers to do two things. First, they provide empowering guidance and promote mutuality and positive partnership. Second, they help couples resolve the issues that led them to seek guidance in the first place. The next five chapters describe, teach, and illustrate each step in turn. We begin with *separating people from problems and passions.*

4

SEPARATING PEOPLE FROM PROBLEMS AND PASSIONS

Rev. Juan Gonzales watched the couple across from him snipe at each other as they had for the past ten minutes, voices rising with each exchange.

"Chris, you know you start most of our fights," said an exasperated Terry. "You just can't stand to let something go by when there's a chance to criticize me."

"And you can't stand to let a moment go by when there's a chance to do something that pisses me off," countered Chris, face turning the shade of an heirloom tomato at the Saturday farmers' market. "I almost feel like you *look* for things to do that you know will drive me up the wall!"

The couple had come for spiritually integrative counseling because they fought about everything, all the time, and felt their behavior did not reflect a "godly relationship." In Chris's words, "It doesn't matter how small the issue is, we end up in an argument about it until we're both so angry we can't even stand to see each other. Terry just won't let up until we're both at the end of our ropes. And that's not how God intended this to be."

After the latest salvo, Juan could see Terry's heartbeat throb in a vein that pulsated in his forehead. "What about the time you intentionally left the dogs outside in the rain so they tracked mud all over the house?" Terry demanded, voice loud enough to startle Chris. "You think I didn't notice that you did that on purpose? You think I didn't notice? You're a sadist—you like to see me suffer."

Juan held his hands up in a T formation.

"Time out," he said. "Let's take a break. I think you're both too physically stimulated right now to listen to each other. We're not making progress here, and we can't until everyone calms down a little."

"Chris started it," Terry said, needing to get in the last word.

"None of that," Juan said, holding up a forefinger. "While we take a break, don't rehearse who's at fault or mull over who said what. You need to clear your minds and let your bodies relax. We'll pick up again in fifteen minutes or so."

He sighed to himself. This wasn't going to be an easy conversation.

A CLOSER LOOK AT THE PROBLEM AND THE PASSION

Terry and Chris identify "fighting" as the primary issue in their relationship, but the passion driving them apart is criticism, the first of Gottman's (1999) Four Horsemen. Criticism is just one aspect of conflict between couples. Conflict can also include high levels of disagreement, stressful and hostile interactions, disrespect, and verbal and physical abuse (Buehler et al. 1998). Emotional distance adds another type of stress to intimate relationships. Some degree of conflict, of course, is necessary to keep a covenant partnership dynamic rather than static (Johnson & Roloff 1998; Ashford, LeCroy, & Lortie 2006). But the sort of ongoing conflict associated with constant criticism can negatively influence many dimensions of a couple's life and the life of the couple's family.

Constant conflict between partners, for example, can contribute to poor mental health (Lian & Geok n.d.; Almeida et al. 2002; Fincham 2003), including depressive symptoms, eating disorders, male alcoholism, and alcohol abuse (Fincham 2003: 23). Children of highly conflicted couples are more likely to have behavioral problems (Von Stutzman 2008). Conflict between partners is also implicated in poor physical health for the couples, including illnesses such as cancer, cardiac disease, chronic pain, and physical injury (Fincham 2003: 23). Finally, more women are murdered each year by their intimate partners than by anyone else.

Criticism and conflict can be harmful and even deadly, in part because they feed on themselves. Criticism usually escalates into defensiveness (it is natural, after all, for a criticized partner to protect herself or himself), which can lead to more criticism, contempt, and stonewalling. Although women tend to be more reactive than men (Almeida et al. 2002), both genders are likely to react to negative behaviors. These behaviors are partly contextual, too: stressful days at work and school tend to lead to more arguments at home, and days with multiple, competing demands on couples—such as holidays—generate more conflict than other days (Fincham 2003: 25).

Criticism on any day, however, can generate a cycle of negativity; people are, in general, less satisfied with life and with their covenant partnerships—and thus more likely to behave negatively—when their partners view them negatively. Likewise, negative verbal interactions like criticism tend to escalate; partners are more likely to repeat negative verbal interactions than positive ones or even negative behavior. This prevents the all-important "rupture and repair" process by which couples recover from criticism, defensiveness, contempt, stonewalling, and other harmful passions to maintain positivity through humor, tolerance, understanding, and empathy.

Breaking the negative cycle of criticism and conflict to increase positivity, goodwill, and mutuality within the covenant friendship is the first intervention a caregiver needs to make. This intervention can begin by *separating people from the problem and passions*, the first step in the SMART approach outlined in chapter 3. Facilitating an externalizing conversation is one way to begin the process.

Externalization places the problem outside of each partner and outside of the relationship, positioning it as something that influences—or even attacks—the couple from beyond. This allows partners to unite against the problem rather than focusing their energies against each other. Externalization is a hallmark of narrative approaches to care; although not required for successful narrative practice (Madigan 2011), it can be helpful more often than not.

INTERNALIZING DISCOURSE VS. EXTERNALIZING CONVERSATIONS

Externalization can be helpful because couples who face a chronic problem like "fighting" can take its ongoing presence—and their inability to get rid of it—as a reflection on who they are as a couple and on each partner as an individual (White & Epston 1990). Often these problem-laden stories are totalizing and pathologizing, and they locate the problem in the identity of the couple or one of the partners. "Persons often come . . . believing that there is something wrong with them producing and perpetuating their predicament: for example, that they possess or incorporate certain faults or inadequacies which mean that they are not capable of living their lives satisfactorily," writes British psychotherapist Martin

Payne (2006: 45). The tenaciousness of the problem—it grows back like crabgrass no matter how many times a couple tries to yank it out—and the couple's failure to eradicate it, confirms for them that negative personal and relational qualities exist "inside" the covenant partnership. The difficulty becomes internalized through a particular, problem-saturated discourse, which renders the problem intractable and nearly impossible to overcome. As a result, hope falters, discouraging the partners and leading to criticism, blame, and defensiveness.

Consider, for example, the way Chris and Terry describe their relationship: they say they fight about everything, all the time, "until we're both so angry we can't even stand to see each other." They have internalized "fighting" as a part of their identity as a couple; it has become a totalizing descriptor of who they are and what they do—so much so that they already know the outcome of a fight before it begins: they will become so angry that they will not be able to look at each other. If we were to externalize this discourse, we might say that the passion of criticism picks a fight between them, invites anger to join in, and then together criticism and anger succeed in pushing Terry and Chris apart until they are unable even to look at each other.

A closer look at the couple's exchange with Reverend Juan illustrates the process of internalization at an individual level, too. Here, each partner is viewed as having an intrinsic fault or inadequacy that contributes to the couple's shared identity as "fighters." In the excerpt below, internalizing discourses are highlighted in bold type, with explanatory notes in italics:

Terry: Chris, you know **you start most of our fights**. (*Criticism that internalizes Chris as "instigator"; "fights" are owned as "ours," something intrinsic to the relationship.*) **You just can't stand to let something go by when there's a chance to criticize me.** (*Criticism that internalizes Chris as "criticizer."*)

Chris: And you can't stand to let a moment go by when there's **a chance to do something that pisses me off**. I almost feel like **you *look* for things to do** that **you know will drive me up the wall!** (*Criticism that internalizes Terry as "opportunist" and "irritator."*)

Terry: What about the time **you intentionally left the dogs outside in the rain** (*criticism that internalizes Chris as "thoughtless"*) so they tracked mud all over the house? You think I didn't notice that **you did that on purpose**? (*Criticism that internalizes Chris as "intentional instigator."*) You think I didn't notice? **You're a sadist— you like to see me suffer.** (*Criticism that internalizes Chris as "sadist" who "enjoys watching Terry suffer."*)

Rev. Juan: Time out. Let's take a break. I think you're both too physically stimulated right now to listen to each other. We're not making progress here, and we can't until everyone calms down a little.

Terry: **Chris started it.** (*Criticism that internalizes Chris as "instigator."*)

To create a space where it is possible for the couple to have a new experience of themselves in relation to the problem, the spiritual caregiver must find a way to create distance between the problem and the identities of the partners. This can be accomplished by helping the couple name the problem in a useful way and by employing language to externalize the problem. Instead of saying that Terry and Chris "fight all the time," for example, a caregiver working from a narrative approach might say that "fighting often finds a way to get Chris and Terry angry with each other." This approach allows people to see themselves in a relationship with a problem that pulls them away from their preferred directions in life. This can shift their entire perspective. As people "perceive themselves in a relationship with a problem (rather than having or being a problem)," writes family therapist William C. Madsen, "they often experience a sense of relief, a bit of distance from the problem, and a greater ability to address the problem" (2007: 9).

Caregivers often understand externalization simply as a therapeutic technique, sort of a linguistic party trick. But it is more than that: it is an attitude, and possessing an externalizing attitude is more important than being able to use externalization as a technique (Freedman & Combs 1996). Think of an externalizing attitude as a stance that the caregiver assumes toward people and problems. This stance allows the caregiver to see discourses, stories, and outside influences where others perceive personalities, qualities, and personal characteristics. To assume this stance, a helper must learn to objectify problems rather than people—a major shift, given the way North American cultures tend to colonize and objectify people through a dominant discourse of deficit and pathology. Madsen describes this stance as a shift from asking, "What caused the problem?" to asking, "What constrains an individual or family from living differently?" (2007: 52). He suggests that externalization offers a "theory of constraints"—an understanding that invites caregivers to carefully examine with couples the forces that constrain them from living together the life that they prefer or want to live. Our task, Madsen says, "becomes one of working with clients to identify constraints and then supporting and assisting them in renegotiating their relationship with constraints" (ibid., 57).

The different assumptions between an externalizing attitude and the dominant discourse are one reason that externalization can be so powerful. Michael White, the originator of narrative therapy, found that

> externalizing opened up possibilities for [families] to describe themselves, each other, and their relationships from a new, non-problem-saturated perspective; it enabled the development of an alternative story of family life, one that was more attractive to family members. From this new perspective, persons were able to locate "facts" about their lives and relationships that could not be even dimly perceived in the problem-saturated account of family life: "facts" that contradicted this problem-saturated accounts; facts that provided the nuclei for the generation of new stories. (White & Epston 1990: 39)

White and his colleague David Epston found that externalization decreases unproductive conflict among family members, undermines a sense of failure in dealing with problems, paves the way for cooperation rather than opposition in facing problems together, opens up new possibilities for action in relation to problems, frees people for a lighter and more effective approach to addressing problems, and presents opportunities for dialogue rather than monologue in relation to problems (1990: 39–40). In short, externalization contributes to mutuality and partnership. It also makes it possible for some people to choose responsibility for the first time for the problems they face (Freedman & Combs 1996).

STARTING TO EXTERNALIZE

Externalization begins by giving the problem a descriptive, relational name. Remember that naming rights belong to the couple! Allowing partners to name their difficulty together—rather than to rely on the caregiver to name it for them—serves the purpose of empowering the couple; it begins to build an alliance between them against the problem, a first step in creating a team allied against the problem. Naming the "demon" gives the couple power over it, just as Jesus gained control over evil spirits by learning their names.

In the naming and externalization process, the problem or passion is characterized as an active agent located outside of the relationship and outside of each individual. The language used in relation to the problem shifts, no longer describing a state of being but instead making it into a thing, an object, or a power that the partners can relate to together. A good way to distinguish internalizing discourse from externalization is to watch for a shift from using adjectives to describe a problem ("You are controlling!" or "Your control needs drive me crazy!") to using a noun to name it ("I hate the way Control runs our relationship!" or "I go nuts when Control makes you do that!").

It is important, however, that the caregiver not rush to externalize the problem. Listen closely to the breadth and complexity of the issues the couple presents (White 2007) before asking them to begin exploring a name (or names) for the difficulties they want to address. The particular name given to a problem is less important than the process of externalization. In fact, psychotherapist Gerald Monk and his colleagues (1997) suggest simply using "it" or "this problem" as a name until a more accurate moniker emerges. The point is that you will develop a more accurate name as you elicit richer information about the problem—and the more accurate the name, the more successful the externalization is apt to become. This is especially true when the internalized discourses causing tension are more cultural than interpersonal—sexism, for example, or homophobia, or stories about what it means to be a man or not to hold a college degree. "Because the habit of thought that constructs these internal understandings of people's lives is significantly a cultural phenomenon," White writes, "many of the problems that people consult therapists about are cultural in nature" (2007: 25). Caregivers should remember this when helping couples name the problems that oppress them.

In exploring the effects of a problem in people's lives, White (2007) suggests that caregivers adopt the posture of an investigative reporter. In particular, the caregiver listens with an "externalizing ear" (Madsen 2007: 190), always converting internalized discourse to externalized relationship. This is accomplished in part by using language that encourages distance from the problem rather than closeness to it.

We can externalize more than "problems," however. We can also externalize unhelpful attitudes, beliefs, actions, meanings, and social roles; internalized discourses that constrain possibilities; and constraining interactions (such as behavioral patterns like criticism-blame-criticism). We should avoid externalizing dangerous, violent, or overtly oppressive behaviors—such as intimate-partner violence, for example, or suicidal thoughts, or the abuse of a child or elderly person. When faced with those issues, spiritual caregivers have an ethical obligation to act to protect and ensure the safety of at-risk persons—not deconstruct the problematic discourses that allow those behaviors to continue.

When externalization is appropriate, however, it can be a powerful ally in empowering couples for significant change. Here are some possible questions that caregivers can use when helping couples name their problems:

- What would you call the issue that pushes you apart?
- What voice is speaking when you argue that way?
- Whose voice is speaking when you argue that way?
- What can we call this thing that gets the two of you so worked up?
- Where did you learn to argue that way? What would you call this way of arguing?
- What's the feeling behind the words? Is that the thing that's calling the shots in your relationship?
- What's the longing you hear behind the criticism?

These questions are guidelines, not set-in-stone rules or standard questions used for externalizing conversations. Creative caregivers will find their own ways to ask about the problems that separate partners, leading couples to externalize and name their demons through uniquely helpful lines of questioning that are appropriate to particular contexts, histories, and situations.

SOOTHING THE BODY'S ALARM SYSTEM

Not much that is productive can be accomplished, however, when the body's alarm system has been activated by criticism and defensiveness. Reverend Juan recognizes that Chris and Terry's bodies have reached the state of diffuse physiological arousal, as indicated by red faces, pulsing veins, and raised voices. As a result, the partners are unlikely to absorb new information, attend to what their partner is saying, or listen carefully to each other. In order to move forward in their conversation, it is essential that they each soothe their body's alarm system, and Rev. Juan has modeled the most important step toward that end: taking a break from difficult conversation.

Teaching couples to take a "time out" for themselves during difficult conversation is one of the most important things caregivers can do. For the best chance of success, a break should have three components (Gottman 1999). First, it should last at least twenty minutes. This is the time needed for a fully aroused body to return to its ordinary, balanced state. Second, a break should be relaxing; partners should soothe themselves with stretching, meditation, reading, or some other activity. They should not spend the time mulling over the fight or situation that caused the physiological arousal in the first place. Third, before partners take a break, they should also schedule a time to come back together to continue the conversation.

A break allows partners to self-soothe and deescalate their physiology. Gottman argues that it is particularly important that men learn to self-soothe, as this ability is one of the best predictors of outcomes in a covenant partnership. He offers five steps to soothing oneself (1999: 232):

- Getting control of breathing by taking smooth, even, deep breaths—about six breaths per minute.

- Noticing areas of tension in the body and intentionally contracting, then relaxing, those muscles.
- Allowing newly relaxed regions to feel heavy, as if weighted down.
- Imagining the relaxed, heavy regions becoming comfortably warm to increase blood flow and induce deep relaxation.
- Imagining a relaxing place or idea—a forest or beach, an image of peace, a favorite color—and entering into it as fully as possible.

Caregivers can teach these five steps to couples anytime the body's alarm system seems to be activated during an empowering conversation.

Note that the practice of self-soothing echoes many aspects of the spiritual virtue of equanimity. Cultivating equanimity on an ongoing basis can be an antidote to both criticism and defensiveness. It allows partners to stay calm and focused despite the presence of two of the Four Horsemen—rooted in an assurance that their integrity is not being challenged and that the relationship is strong and safe despite the ways in which the passions are assailing it at any given moment.

NAMING DEMONS WITH TERRY AND CHRIS

Once Terry and Chris had soothed themselves and returned their bodies to a calm, balanced state, Rev. Juan gently reintroduced the topic at hand.

"Before our break," he began, "I heard a lot of criticism, a lot of blaming—you were defending yourselves from each other a lot, too. I get why you say you fight all the time. If I assume you're on good behavior here in my office, I can imagine that the fights at home must be pretty intense!"

"Boy, are they!" Chris concurred. Terry nodded agreement.

"They push you apart pretty quickly," Juan continued. "They really get you to turn on each other. You're like two pit bulls lunging against your chains." (*Notice the subtle way Juan uses externalizing language to describe what the fights do to the couple.*)

"That's not how I want to be," admitted Terry. "But when Chris starts in, I—"

"Nope," Juan said, holding up his palm. "We're not going to do criticism and blame right now. I want us to find a way to describe what this thing is that pushes you apart."

"What do you mean?" Chris asked.

"I mean, what do we call this power, this force, that gets you to turn on each other with so much energy?" Juan asked. (*Here, Juan overtly introduces the idea of externalizing by naming the problem as a "power" or "force" that acts on the couple by harnessing the energy of the partners.*)

"Fighting," Terry said. "It's fighting."

"Tell me more about The Fighting." (*Here, Juan shifts from using the professional terms* criticism *and* blame *to the colloquial term* fighting. *It mirrors the language used by the couple, and he adds distance by using the article* the, *as in "The Fighting.")*

"Well," Chris said. "We fight. It just happens."

"Really?" Juan asked. "Or is 'fighting' what this force gets you to do with each other?" (*Juan does not accept the first, "thin" description of the fights, but invites them to say more by asking them to look for constraining elements that lead to The Fighting.*)

"You mean fighting is a symptom?" Chris asked.

"Maybe," Juan said, nodding. "What do you hear behind the words of your arguments?" (*Again, he invites them to identify constraining elements that lead to The Fighting.*)

"Well," Terry said, "Chris gets so angry."

✓ "And Terry gets so blaming," Chris said. "Like he's the only one who suffers, and I'm the only thing in the world that causes suffering for him."

"So there are three good candidates," Juan said, chuckling. "It could be Anger; could be Blame; could be Suffering. Do any of those seem on target?" The couple was silent for a moment. "Maybe not," Juan continued. "What bothers you most about The Fighting?"

"I hate how disrespectful Chris sounds," Terry said.

"So Disrespect is at work behind the scenes?" Juan asked. (*Juan continues to turn adjectives into nouns, externalizing the qualities that the couples names as problematic.*)

"I guess," Terry shrugged.

"It is for me, definitely," Chris said. "I don't feel like Terry would criticize me so much if there were any respect in our relationship."

"So for you, Disrespect gets Terry to criticize you?" Juan inquired. Chris nodded.

"What bothers you about Disrespect, Terry?" Juan asked.

"Well . . . people who love each other aren't supposed to act like that," Terry responded, blushing slightly. "They are supposed to love and cherish each other. When Chris talks in ways that are disrespectful, I start to wonder if this marriage really has as much love in it as I used to believe it did."

"So the Disrespect makes you doubt the love in your relationship," Juan commented. Terry and Chris both nodded. "And when you doubt the love, you get scared and angry?" They both nodded again. Juan allowed silence to settle in the room for a few moments. "Could it be," he ventured gently, "that 'Disrespect' is that power we've been trying to name?"

"Yes," Chris and Terry said together, then laughed.

"Jinx!" said Chris.

Juan laughed with them. "Maybe we should explore Disrespect a little bit next time we get together. Would that seem like a fruitful way to spend our time?"

TRY IT YOURSELF

To taste the consequences of internalizing and externalizing discourses, answer the following questions based on an exercise by narrative psychotherapists Jill Freedman and Gene Combs (1996: 49–50).

First, identify a quality about yourself that causes you dissatisfaction. Maybe you are angry more often than you would like. Maybe you tend to be too hard on yourself. Maybe you overwork or procrastinate or are too critical of others. Don't make it something so serious that you will have trouble getting through the exercise; just make it something that causes mild discomfort from time to time. Every time you encounter a _____ in the questions, use the quality you have identified.

INTERNALIZING QUESTIONS

- How long have you been _____?
- How did you become _____?
- What causes you to remain _____?

- How does being _____ benefit you?
- How does being _____ harm you or detract from you life?
- What difficulties in your life come from being _____?
- How hopeful are you that you can overcome _____ in your life?

Take a deep breath. What feelings did the internalizing questions awaken in you? How did they make you feel about yourself? How hopeful are you after answering the questions? Note the level of energy in your body and the sort of self-talk going through your mind. Then take a short break—stretch, get a drink of water, walk around the room a couple of times.

Now change the quality you identified into a noun. For example, if you chose "angry," make it "anger"; if you chose "critical," make it "criticism"; and so on. Substitute the noun form of your identified quality for the _____ in the following questions.

EXTERNALIZING QUESTIONS

- How long has _____ influenced you?
- How did _____ come to influence you?
- What causes you to remain under the influence of _____?
- How does the presence of _____ benefit you?
- How does the presence of _____ harm you or detract from your life?
- How does _____ create difficulties in your life?
- How hopeful are you that you can relate differently to _____ in your life?

Take a deep breath. What feelings did the externalizing questions awaken in you? How did they make you feel about yourself? How hopeful are you after answering the questions? Note the level of energy in your body and the sort of self-talk going through your mind. Then take a short break—stretch, get a drink of water, walk around the room a couple of times.

IMPLICATIONS FOR SPIRITUAL CARE
AND COUNSELING

When the destructive passion of criticism attacks a couple, a spiritual caregiver seeks to counteract its effects by increasing positivity and equanimity. One way to begin this process is to separate the couple from the problem by listening with an externalizing ear during an externalizing conversation. At the same time, caregivers must remember the organic wholeness of human beings and attend to embodiment by deescalating physical arousal so that meaningful communication can occur. It is difficult to listen to each other when physiological alarm bells are ringing and behavior and interpretation are partly determined by physiology. Teaching couples to self-soothe may be a necessary step in order for externalization to occur.

Separating the couple from the problem and the passion helps to depathologize the situation, empowering the partners in the face of their difficulty and awakening hope that they can relate differently to the situation, attitude, roles, or other constraints holding them back from the life they prefer. To empower couples in this way, caregivers must stand in solidarity with the couple as a team allied against the difficulty at work to separate them. This standing-in-solidarity-with is analogous to the ancient mode of sustaining care.

Finally, viewing externalization as a theory of constraints—the idea that certain biological, personal, familial, social, and sociocultural stories, powers, and forces keep people from living fully the lives that they prefer—broadens spiritual care beyond a focus on the individual to account for the way couples are embedded in systems of meaning beyond their control. This allows caregivers and the couples they seek to empower to engage in some degree of cultural critique. Doing so can increase their freedom by allowing them to relate differently to—and perhaps experience liberation from—oppressive cultural beliefs, attitudes, roles, and practices.

In order for this increase of freedom to occur, couples and their caregivers must first have a fuller understanding of the influence of problems on the lives of the partners—and of the partners' influence on the lives of problems. We turn our attention to this in chapter 5.

5

MAPPING MUTUAL INFLUENCE

When Janice and Manuel married eight years ago, they agreed to do whatever it took to support each other's dreams of success in the corporate world. And it worked—Manuel cooked dinner and changed diapers while Janice climbed the hierarchy of her financial-sector career; Janice worked weekends to pay for Manuel's evening MBA program. Together they negotiated the pluses and minuses of various life decisions, celebrating each tiny success. Today they are respected managers who remain valuable to their companies despite recent economic changes, including falling profits and the layoff of other employees. Now in their late thirties, they have two sons, five-year-old Sam and three-year-old Beau, a beautiful home, aging parents, and a serious marital crisis. "We've got to change something," Janice says, "or the whole family is going to implode."

The problem, named in their first conversation with a spiritually integrative counselor, is imbalance. "Life's just too much of a good thing," Manuel says. "We can't hold it all together—there's always something else that needs to be done at work, at home, with the boys, let alone with our marriage. We're both just exhausted by the end of the day."

Today, at their second conversation with the counselor, each feels blamed by the other for the state of their lives and the state of their marriage.

"Well, I have a right to be exhausted," Janice says with a sigh. "I commute for ninety minutes, work ten hours, drive home again, and then I work another three hours to keep the house picked up, bathe the boys, read to them, get them to sleep, make sure laundry gets done. I don't even stop to breathe. Last night I found myself cleaning the bathtub while still in the heels I wore to work!"

Manuel crossed his arms. "I'm sorry I didn't clean the tub, honey. But by the time I picked up the boys from day care and got dinner ready for them, there was barely enough time to mow the yard while it was still light outside. I needed to check on Mom and Dad. And then you were home, and I wanted to spend time with you, and . . ."

"Don't pin this on me," Janice said sharply, shaking her head. "It's not my fault you feel overworked." She sighed again. "The bathtub's not your responsibility anyway," she offered in a gentler tone. "There's just too much going on every day. Maybe we should move so we can start over with a clean house!" The couple laughed together.

Despite their laughter, however, they face a painful and potentially harmful situation.

A CLOSER LOOK AT THE PROBLEM AND THE PASSION

Janice and Manuel have named their difficulty "imbalance," referring to the difficulty of balancing work and other life responsibilities, like household management, children, elder care, leisure, and maintaining their own connection. Their words and body language suggest that the passion of defensiveness is at work in their communication; they seem to interpret each other—or some unknown entity—as critical about the ways they both fail to measure up to the ideal of "having it all" with ease and comfort. (Cultural stories communicated through commercials, films, television shows, and other media often establish unrealistic expectations, which couples then measure themselves against, even as they acknowledge the standard as unattainable.)

The question of work-life balance—also called work-family conflict—is a significant one in the United States. One study reports that 44 percent of U.S. workers were overworked at some time in 2004, and one-third of all U.S. workers were chronically overworked (Galinsky et al. 2005). A decade later, those numbers are likely to have increased; responsibilities and hours worked have grown after the downsizing and layoffs that followed the 2008 economic crisis and consequent financial recession. In addition, few U.S. Americans use the vacation time they earn. The United States is the only advanced economy in the world that does not guarantee its workers paid vacation—in fact, one in four U.S. Americans receives no vacation days—and most workers receive an average of only thirteen to fifteen vacation days per year (compared to at least twenty paid vacation days and as many as thirty or more in

European countries; Ray & Schmitt 2007). Yet fewer than two-thirds of U.S. Americans use all of their vacation time.

Time can be one of the primary factors in work-family conflict, as it appears to be for Janice and Manuel. Time-based conflict occurs when there are simply not enough hours to accomplish all of one's responsibilities at work and in the family. Work-family conflict can also be strain based, in which pressures at work create problems at home (or vice versa), or behavior based, in which the role a person plays at work—"assertive, nonempathetic boss," for example—continues at home and creates relational difficulties (see Hammer & Thompson 2003). Work-family conflict of all types is worse for couples who care for children, dependent parents, or others (Hammer & Thompson 2003; Bianchi & Milkie 2010). In fact, about half of all parents experience significant work-life conflict (Bianchi & Milkie 2010). In short, as one team of scholars studying the contemporary family noted, "Mothers have joined fathers in the work force, the average workweek has been extended, parents spend less time with children . . . , and married couples spend less time with each other" (Browning et al. 1997: 316).

These conflicts are not benign. People who experience significant difficulties with work-life balance report decreased satisfaction in all areas of life, as well as poorer mental and physical health (Hammer & Thompson 2003). Physical symptoms include strain, depression, and burnout (Bianchi & Milkie 2010). Thirty-six percent of those who are highly overworked are also highly stressed, and 21 percent report depressive symptoms (Galinsky et al. 2005). Headaches, fatigue, irritability, and sleepiness can all be symptoms of work-family conflict, and overworked individuals are less likely to take good care of themselves (ibid.). Work performance suffers, too, with lower productivity, higher absenteeism, greater numbers of errors, and higher resentment against employers and coworkers (ibid.).

The difficulties presented by overwork, and the accompanying struggle for work-life balance, are so damaging to families that a team of theologians recommended in 1997 that religious communities and policymakers advocate for a shared workweek not exceeding a total of sixty hours for parents with young children. That is, the parents should work a combined total of no more than sixty hours per week. "There is evidence that the happiest families are those in which both husband and wife have some paid employment, share household chores and child care, and work less than two full-time positions," the team wrote. "Churches, in their theologies of work and leisure, should support such arrangements" (Browning et al. 1997: 316).

Gender makes a difference. Women generally report higher levels of conflict among their roles (Bianchi & Milkie 2010), and more women than men spend time on cleaning and other household activities. For example, on an average day in 2010, 84 percent of women and 67 percent of men spent some time cleaning, cooking, doing lawn care, or taking care of finances, or other household management tasks (BLS 2011). Both genders spent about the same amount of time on their tasks, but 20 percent of men and 48 percent of women did housework, while 41 percent of men and 68 percent of women cooked or cleaned up after a meal. Household duties do not appear to be evenly shared among U.S. heterosexual couples. No wonder Janice and Manuel seem defensive!

Defensiveness can lead to contempt and stonewalling. Breaking this negative cycle to increase positivity, goodwill, and mutuality within the covenant friendship requires a caregiver to *map mutual influence*, the second step in the SMART approach. Mapping mutual influence begins once the problem and passion have been separated from the couple. It recognizes that the problem and passion have particular influences—behavioral, cognitive, spiritual, interactional, interpretive—over each partner and over the couple as a team. It also recognizes that the couple has influence on the problem and the passion. Mapping these influences helps the couple, over time, develop more fluid descriptions of the problem. This can liberate them to view their situation in new ways. Mapping the influence of the couple helps to shape their identity as a team aligned against the problem. This can solidify externalization and reduce conflict and defensiveness over which partner is responsible for the problem, so that partners can unite against it rather than fight against each other.

MAPPING CONVERSATIONS VS. ORDINARY CONVERSATIONS

Couples who face ongoing challenges like "imbalance" and "defensiveness" can feel as if the challenges are always in control. The challenges become a monolithic presence in the couple's life. Like a mountain range seen from a great distance, they can seem solid, impenetrable, omnipresent, almost omnipotent, as if there is never a moment when they are not present and in control—even if they are simply lurking in the background. Mapping the influence of the challenges allows the couple to learn the terrain, tendencies, and habits of their problems. By "influence," I mean the effects that a problem or passion has on the relationships, identities, agency, and roles of the couple as a team and of the partners as individuals. Mapping influence allows couples to identify when defensiveness comes out at night and where it feeds, for example; through mapping, imbalance reveals its weaknesses, and how it protects against them; mapping allows the couple to learn the protective coloring that camouflages both the problems and the passions stalking the partners through the territory of everyday life. Thus the mountain range that seemed insurmountable begins to unfold gradually, revealing the passes and canyons that allow safe passage.

Likewise, mapping the influence of the couple over the challenges allows the partners to glimpse the times when they are able to subdue the problem and resist the passion, or find a fresh path through inhospitable landscape, asserting their agency despite the presence of the Powers.

Ordinary conversation, on the other hand, reifies the problem and the passion through totalizing language. It reinforces the couple's sense of helplessness by emphasizing the broad presence of the challenges they face, making the Powers seem insurmountable. It hides the systemic nature of the Powers and causes people to believe that the problem lies in their own deficits, not in problematic social expectations and discourses. As a result, defensiveness becomes a default position as people seek to protect themselves from the blame they expect from partners and project onto themselves from the cultural stories and expectations surrounding them.

Consider, for example, the way that Janice and Manuel talk to each other about their difficulties: they do not acknowledge the feelings behind the words but respond defensively to perceived criticisms from each other. The passion of defensiveness keeps them from connecting at an emotional level and at the level of content; each is unable to affirm the exhaustion and overload the other is feeling. "Imbalance" has affected not only their external behaviors, but also their inner life as a couple. It keeps them separated from each other, unable to connect at a more satisfying level. (Nonetheless, Janice and Manuel show evidence of being able to repair this distance when she makes a joke about their predicament and they both laugh, momentarily bridging the distance between them and strengthening the covenant friendship.) If we were to map this discourse, we might say that the problem of imbalance and the passion of defensiveness gang up on the couple, keeping them apart until Janice manages to use humor to fend them off and reconnect with Manuel for a moment. This might give the couple the energy to resist the passion and the problem for a while, making an even stronger connection and solidifying the covenant friendship despite the often overbearing presence of defensiveness.

A closer look at the couple's exchange shows just how much imbalance and defensiveness wield power in the conversation. Each partner seems almost unaware of the other, responding instead to a felt sense of criticism that is not explicitly present. It is almost as if defensiveness keeps them from hearing accurately. In the excerpt below, defensive discourses are highlighted in **bold** type, with *explanatory notes* in italics:

Janice: **I have a right to be exhausted.** (*No one has said that Janice has no right to feel exhausted, but she feels a need to defend her fatigue. The sense of fatigue is one of the influences of imbalance that could be identified through a mapping conversation.*) I commute for ninety minutes, work ten hours, drive home again, and then I work another three hours to keep the house picked up, bathe the boys, read to them, get them to sleep, make sure laundry gets done. (*This litany qualifies as a* complaint, *not as* criticism, *because it is focused on herself and not on Manuel.*) **I don't even stop to breathe.** Last night I found myself cleaning the bathtub while still in the heels I wore to work! (*Both of these sentences are effects of imbalance that could be identified through a mapping conversation.*)

Manuel: **I'm sorry I didn't clean the tub, honey.** (*Defensiveness leads him to hear her* complaint *about cleaning the tub in dress shoes as* criticism, *and he responds with a defensive apology. A mapping conversation could help identify this as an effect of the passion of defensiveness.*) **But by the time I picked up the boys from day care and got dinner ready for them, there was barely enough time to mow**

the yard while it was still light outside. I needed to check on Mom and Dad. And then you were home, and I wanted to spend time with you, and . . . (*Manuel's litany is both a* complaint *about his busyness and a* defense *against the critique he has interpreted from Janice's words. Again, a mapping conversation could help identify this as an influence of the passion.*)

Janice: **Don't pin this on me. It's not my fault you feel overworked.** (*Again, defensiveness has caused Janice to interpret Manuel's words as a criticism. A mapping conversation could identify this as an effect of imbalance and defensiveness.*) The bathtub's not your responsibility anyway. There's just too much going on every day. Maybe we should move so we can start over with a clean house! (*With these three sentences, Janice makes a repair attempt; she invites the couple to make a positive turn in their exchange to strengthen the covenant friendship rather than continuing their defensiveness. A mapping conversation would identify this as an example of Janice's influence over defensiveness and perhaps over imbalance.*)

Both: *Laughter.* (*The laughter suggests that Manuel received and responded positively to Janice's repair attempt; this tells us that her influence over defensiveness and imbalance has succeeded. This is something to note in a mapping conversation to highlight the couple's sense of agency in what feels like a powerless situation.*)

To map mutual influence, a caregiver methodically explores the couple's life and relationships to become intimate with the tactics and means of operating that problems and passions use in their interactions with the partners (as individuals and as a team). We now turn to that task, exploring first what dimensions of life are mapped, then the processes of mapping, and finally, questions helpful to the mapping endeavor.

BEGINNING TO MAP MUTUAL INFLUENCE

Mapping mutual influence requires that caregivers trust expert guides—the couples with whom they care—to teach them the strategies that problems and passions use to separate partners and keep them apart. Rather than *being* the problem, the couple has a relationship with the problem (see Freedman & Combs 1996: 66), and one value of mapping conversations is that they allow people to recognize, evaluate, and renegotiate their relationships with problems and passions (Madigan 2011: 283).

As you will see, in many ways, the questions used in mapping mutual influences overlap with the externalization process; the first two phases of the SMART approach mutually reinforce each other in a circular pattern: an externalization question leads to a mapping question, which leads to an externalizing question, and so forth. "During this process," psychotherapist Michael White notes, "people become aware of the fact that they do possess a certain know-how that can be further developed and used to guide them in their effort to address their problems and predicaments" (2007: 43).

Anticipating the Terrain to Be Mapped

Before attempting to map mutual influences, caregivers must anticipate what terrain will be explored through the process. Two domains of experience are explored, along two particular axes, during mapping processes.

The two domains of experience are life—everything that a couple experiences—and relationships. The domain of life, as articulated by White (2007: 43), includes roles (home, work, school, peers, parents, lovers, and other contexts), identity, and eschatology (future possibilities and life horizons). The domain of relationships includes family relationships, friendships, peer relationships, a person's relationship with herself or himself (ibid.), and the partners' relationships with Spirit.

These domains occupy two axes—the *meaning* axis, which identifies the meanings a couple attributes to particular events or situations, and the *action* axis, which identifies the impact of events or situations on a couple's behaviors. In general, I encourage caregivers to map the meaning of an experience before mapping the actions that have resulted. This ensures that the caregiver attends to the *perception* dimension of experience that is so important to Gottman's theory of relational change.

Mapping is accomplished through curiosity-driven questions in each domain, directed first toward one axis and then to the other. Questions along the meaning axis seek to uncover interior understandings of events and situations. For example, what does it mean that something happened to this couple in particular and not to another? Why would God choose them for this particular experience? What responsibilities does the event place on the couple? How has the experience changed the couple's understandings of their partnership? Of covenant? What does it say about the couple that they were open to the experience? What was God calling them to through this experience? What prepared the couple for this particular event? What biblical character's experience is closest to this couple's experience? How would the couple's friends, parents, children, or coworkers feel about the experience? How would they look at the couple differently as a result of it?

Questions along the action axis seek to identify how the experience has affected the couple's behaviors. How has their prayer life changed, for example? Who have they told about the experience? How does the couple relate differently to God and to other people as a result of the event? What religious or spiritual activities have resulted from the experience? What changes have the partners noticed in their thoughts, feelings, and actions? How did they respond to the experience in prayer or ritual? How does the couple hope to be different at work or church, in the choir or at baseball practice, as a result of this experience? How do they imagine other people have responded to similar experiences?

Structuring a Mapping Conversation

A mapping conversation follows a basic structure that assists caregivers in identifying the influence of problems and passions in the life of a couple, as well as the influence of a couple in the life of a problem or passion. Essentially, the caregiver uses curiosity-driven questions to map the effects of the problem on the couple (including the consequent losses it causes) and the couple's role in the life of the problem (and the consequent gains they see). Then the caregiver uses questions to help the couple evaluate the effects of the problem or passion on their life and to justify their evaluation of those effects.

Mapping the Influence of Problems and Passions. Caregivers begin to map mutual influence by first asking how problems and passions shape the daily life of the couple together and of the partners as individuals. This helps achieve a mutual understanding of the problem-saturated situation that is close to the couple's experience (Madigan 2011: 87). This part of the process takes time; it is important that caregivers move slowly through asking about the effects of the problem and passion on the life of the couple. The questions asked should be questions that you could not possibly know the answers to already, and they should leave no area of the couple's life or relationships unexamined. Thoroughly explore both the axis of meaning and the axis of action.

Helpful questions[1] at this stage of the process can include the following:

- How does this problem or passion show up in your work life? In your life outside of work? In your life as a couple? In your bedroom? At the dinner table? In your friendships? When you go out with friends?
- What kind of behaviors does this problem or passion recruit you into? How does it get you to act toward your partner? Toward your covenant partnership? What is its purpose in doing this to you?
- What does this problem or passion get you to think about yourselves as a couple? As a partner? As parents?
- When this problem or passion is having its way with you, what happens to your dreams for the future? (Madigan 2011: 88)
- What dissatisfies you most about the problem or passion's relationship to you and your partner? To your relationships with others?
- How has this problem or passion affected your relationship with yourself?
- If you developed a closer, more intimate relationship with this problem or passion, how would that affect your future as a couple?
- What has this problem or passion promoted in your relationship?
- How does this problem or passion worm its way between the two of you? (Freedman & Combs 1996: 124)
- What ways of life does this problem or passion ride piggy-back on? (ibid.)
- What have you lost as a result of this problem or passion? What has it cost you?

Mapping a Couple's Role in the Life of the Problem. It is important for partners to see that their relationship with the problem and passion entails mutuality; not only do the problem and passion have effects on the couple, but the couple has a role in maintaining the life of the problem. Questions that reveal the couple's role—the sorts of things that they think, feel, and do that give power to the problem and passion—help partners begin to see themselves as authors of their lives. This can enhance their sense of agency. It also allows caregivers to begin to see the habitual—and passionate, in the spiritual sense—ways that couples talk about or frame their relationship to a problem and passion.

Useful questions for this phase of the process can include:

- How does this problem or passion convince you that you can't do anything about it (Nylund 2000: 90)? What other problems or passions are its friends?
- When does this problem or passion have the easiest time getting to you? When does it have a really hard time getting to you?
- What does this problem or passion whisper to you? How does it manage to be so convincing?
- What ideas, thoughts, feelings, habits, and behaviors feed or encourage the problem or passion?
- Are there ways that you have unknowingly given the problem or passion the upper hand in your life as a couple? (Madigan 2011: 88)
- Have there been people or situations in your life that have helped you keep the problem or passion central to your life? (ibid.)
- Who benefits from the problem or passion having so much power in your relationship? Whose interests are being served when the problem or passion has so much influence?
- What sort of people would proudly advocate for the problem or passion? What groups of people would definitely be opposed to it? (Freedman & Combs, 1996: 68)
- What attitudes must be present to justify the behaviors that the problem or passion elicits from you?
- What experiences have you had in the past that encourage these ways of responding to the problem or passion?

- When in history did these sorts of ideas gain prominence? How were they used? How did you learn of them? (Freedman & Combs 1996: 123)

White says that introducing these sorts of inquiries "provides people with an opportunity to define their own position in relation to their problems and to give voice to what underpins this position" (2007: 39). In the process, they redefine not only their relationship to problems and passions but also to each other. By listening to and acknowledging each other's point of view, couples can develop a stronger, shared sense of identity that nurtures the covenant friendship and "fosters a more relational sense of identity" (ibid., 59).

Evaluating Effects and Justifying the Evaluation. Once the couple and caregiver have thoroughly mapped both the effects of the problem or passion and the role of the couple in the life of the problem or passion, it is time to evaluate what has been learned through the mapping process. The caregiver begins the evaluation by summarizing what the mapping has revealed; for example, "So, we identified that defensiveness causes both of you to lash out at each other and then withdraw. We also found out that withdrawing feeds the defensiveness, because you nurse your wounds and rehearse the injuries you receive from each other, which just gives the defensiveness more strength the next time you argue."

After the summary, the caregiver invites an evaluation of these effects with questions such as these:

- Given what we've learned about the problem or the passion, how helpful is its presence in your relationship?
- With these sorts of effects, what's the overall influence of the problem or passion on the sort of partnership you'd like to have?
- What are the costs and benefits of relating to the problem or passion in this way?
- What do you gain from having this sort of relationship to the problem or passion?
- What do you lose from having this sort of relationship to the problem or passion?

These questions invite people to pause and reflect on their relationships to the problems and passions. It is important that once a couple has evaluated the effects of these relationships, they be asked to justify their evaluations by providing reasons for their opinions and evidence to support them. The process of justifying their evaluations allows them to voice their preferred ways of being and to begin developing new ideas about how they would like to live together as a couple. Questions that help a couple justify their evaluations can include the following:

- What evidence supports your evaluation?
- If you maintain this sort of relationship to the problem or passion, what do you imagine happening to your partnership in the future?
- What would you like to happen to your partnership instead of the effects that you've evaluated this way?
- What thoughts, feelings, or actions could grow out of this evaluation?

INCREASING POSITIVE EXCHANGES

Mapping mutual influence makes positive exchanges more likely by helping couples see how habitual their responses to problems and passions have become—and how simple it can be to make small changes that reduce the effects of the problems and passions in their lives. Small, positive behaviors—such as the way Janice uses humor to interrupt the cycle of defensiveness while she and Manuel are talking with their counselor—repeated often can make a big difference in a partnership. "When both partners commit to making small but consistently positive shifts in their interactions, they can take their marriage to a much happier place. And it's easier to assimilate small changes, rather than big ones" (Gottman, Gottman, & DeClaire 2006: 7).

Four behaviors, in particular, contribute to increasingly positive exchanges (Gottman 1999; Gottman, Gottman, & DeClaire 2006). First, partners should strive for "softened start-up." This means beginning to talk about a problem gently, without criticizing, defending, or showing contempt. When a conversation begins softly, the other partner is more likely to listen and understand what is being said.

Second, partners should work at turning toward each other—that is, demonstrating that they are open, listening, and paying attention to each other. The other options are turning away—ignoring what their partners are saying—or turning against their partners by allowing anger, sarcasm, criticism, or other harsh responses to set the tone for the exchange. Turning toward each other during conversation is the first and most positive behavior couples can use to set the stage for a productive exchange in which the problem or passion has less effect on their communication.

Third, when communication becomes tense or difficult—when the Four Horsemen arrive in force or when the passion and problem take control of the conversation—couples can make (and accept) repair attempts. A repair attempt can be a smile, a gentle joke, an apology, a compliment, or any other interaction that breaks the tension and allows each partner to relax a little bit. (When one partner makes a repair attempt, it is important that the other receive the attempt by acknowledging and building on it.)

Finally, accepting influence from each other is especially effective in creating a positive climate for conversation. This means each partner is willing to be persuaded by the other, rather than trying to dominate the relationship or stubbornly holds on to an opinion. Gottman's research (1999) suggests it is especially helpful to a strong covenant friendship when a man is willing to accept influence from his female partner—the way Manuel did when Janice made a joke.

MAPPING THE TERRITORY WITH JANICE AND MANUEL

When Janice and Manuel finished laughing about moving to a new, clean house, their counselor gave them a quizzical look. "Well," she said, grinning, "relocation might be one solution. But I'm curious about what would happen if Imbalance moved with you. How would you know it was there?" (*She continues to externalize Imbalance, beginning to map its effects by asking how the couple would notice its presence in a new home.*)

"Oh, that's easy," Janice said. "We'd still snipe at each other, still feel exhausted, still run around feeling like there was always something we hadn't managed to finish." Manuel nodded. (*Janice names some behavioral and affective effects of Imbalance.*)

"Hmm," said the counselor. "How would you describe those feelings that Imbalance triggers in both of you?" (*Now the counselor asks a question along the axis of meaning, hoping to help each partner hear the inner effects of Imbalance and thus begin to tell a shared story about its effects.*)

"Makes me feel like I'm not enough," Manuel said. "Like everybody else can handle life but me."

"Same for me," agreed Janice. "I feel pretty inadequate." (*The couple begins to articulate a shared story about inadequacy, insufficiency, and not measuring up to others.*)

"And what does Imbalance whisper to you that brings forth those feelings?" asked the counselor. (*Continuing to externalize, the counselor stays with the axis of meaning with a question that seeks more detail about the inner effects of Imbalance on the couple.*)

"You mean, what do I hear in my head that makes me feel that way?" asked Manuel. The counselor nodded. The couple sat in silence for a minute.

"It tells me that there's something wrong with me," Janice said. "That I need to try harder, work harder, if I want to have a life like I see on television." (*Janice clearly articulates a negative effect of Imbalance—the messages she receives from it, including the message that she's at fault for the problems she is experiencing.*)

"For me it's not so much that I need to work harder," said Manuel. "It's that if I just find balance, everything will fall into place— that I ought to be able to do it all if I'm really the kind of guy I want to be." (*Manuel also articulates a negative effect of Imbalance—that it keeps him from being the type of guy he wants to be, and that it tells him he is responsible for finding balance on his own. Now the counselor has some indication of the strong forces keeping this couple apart from each other—each partner feels like a failure, to some extent, and has taken some unrealistic responsibility for the tension in the relationship.*)

The counselor nodded. "I wonder whose interests it serves for you to keep those dissatisfying messages at the front of your mind?" she asked gently. (*Here the counselor begins to map the couple's role in the life of the problem by asking whose needs are being met when they collude with Imbalance.*)

"I don't know," Janice said. "But it sure doesn't serve the best interests of our kids—or us. I don't even *want* to have a life like I see on television. But I feel like I *should* want that life. Maybe that's what got us into this mess—trying to have the 'American dream' instead of dreams of our own." (*Janice avoids the hard work of identifying the cultural stories that are influencing her marriage but moves toward evaluating the effects of Imbalance on her partnership—it's something that's not in the best interests of her family and perhaps not even congruent with what they want for themselves.*)

"Baby, I thought this life *was* your dream," Manuel said. "I thought it was *our* dream. But it sure doesn't feel like what I thought I was signing on for when we used to talk about the future." (*Manuel begins to agree with Janice's evaluation, voicing his own dissatisfaction. Together they are beginning to hear each other's feelings and to understand unspoken frustrations and dreams. In the process, they are beginning to write a shared story together about their life as a couple in a relationship with Imbalance, rather than each responding harshly in response to the power of Imbalance and its attendant passion, defensiveness.*)

This brief illustration of a mapping conversation—in which the process of thoroughly tracking Imbalance in the lives of Janice and Manuel barely begins—demonstrates the power of this stage of the SMART approach. Mapping, coupled with separating the couple from problems and passions, can quickly allow partners to hear and understand each other differently, building a rich understanding of how the problem effects their life together inwardly and outwardly. The new, shared story that emerges provides a springboard for identifying, building, and attending to teamwork in the next stage of the model.

TRY IT YOURSELF

To experience the effects of a mapping conversation, explore the following questions for yourself. First, return to the quality about yourself that you identified in chapter 4 as causing dissatisfaction—the one that causes you mild discomfort from time to time. Every time you encounter a _____ in the questions, fill in the blank with the quality you have identified.

MAPPING THE EFFECTS OF THE PROBLEM OR PASSION

- How does _____ show up in your work life? In your life outside of work? At the dinner table? In your friendships?
- What kind of behaviors does _____ recruit you into? How does it get you to act toward your partner? Toward your covenant partnership? What is its purpose in doing this to you?
- When _____ is having its way with you, what happens to your dreams for the future?
- How has _____ affected your relationship with yourself?
- What has _____ promoted in your relationship?
- What ways of life does _____ ride piggyback on?
- What have you lost as a result of _____? What has it cost you?

Take a deep breath. What feelings did these mapping questions awaken in you? How did they make you feel about your relationship to the quality you identified? How hopeful are you after answering the questions? Note the level of energy in your body and the sort of self-talk going through your mind. Then take a short break—stretch, get a drink of water, walk around the room a couple of times.

MAPPING YOUR ROLE IN THE LIFE OF THE PROBLEM OR PASSION

Now answer these questions about the role you play in the life of the quality you identified:

- How does _____ convince you that you can't do anything about it? What other problems or passions are its friends?
- When does _____ have the easiest time getting to you? When does it have a really hard time getting to you?
- What does _____ whisper to you? How does it manage to be so convincing?
- What ideas, thoughts, feelings, habits, and behaviors feed or encourage _____?

- Are there ways that you have unknowingly given _____ the upper hand in your life?
- Have there been people or situations in your life that have helped you keep _____ central to your life?
- Who benefits from _____ having so much power in your life? Whose interests are being served when _____ has so much influence?
- What attitudes must be present to justify the behaviors that _____ elicits from you? When in history did these sorts of ideas gain prominence? How were they used? How did you learn of them?
- What experiences have you had in the past that encourage these ways of responding to the _____?

Take a deep breath. What feelings did these mapping questions about your role in sustaining the quality awaken? How did they make you feel about your relationship to the quality you identified? How hopeful are you after answering the questions? Note the level of energy in your body and the sort of self-talk going through your mind. Then take a short break—stretch, get a drink of water, walk around the room a couple of times.

Finally, what is your evaluation of the effects of _____ on your life? What evidence can you offer to justify your evaluation? What would you like to have present instead of the effects you have identified through mapping?

IMPLICATIONS FOR SPIRITUAL CARE AND COUNSELING

When the destructive passion of defensiveness and the challenge of work-life balance are at work to separate a couple, a spiritual caregiver begins to bring the partners together by increasing positivity and beginning to create a shared story about the couple's relationship to imbalance. This process begins by mapping mutual influence—identifying the effects of the problem and passion on the couple and the role of the couple in the life of the problem and passion. At the same time, caregivers must remember the importance of teaching the couple about turning toward each other with gentleness. It is difficult to resist defensiveness when harsh speech, stimulated by stress and imbalance, has become a norm within a relationship.

Breaking this pattern through the mapping of mutual influence also helps to solidify the externalization of problems and passions, allowing couples to achieve a mutual understanding of their situation and to see themselves as authors (or coauthors) of their own stories. It can also enhance their sense of agency. Throughout this process, caregivers remain in solidarity with the couple, allied as a team against the Powers working to separate the partners. As mentioned in chapter 4, this standing-in-solidarity-with is analogous to the ancient mode of sustaining care. As mapping begins to empower the couple, however, the caregiver moves steadily toward a stance more analogous to the ancient mode of guiding care—that of empowering them to act toward agency and justice. When mapping questions are woven together skillfully, they invite couples to retell their stories in a way that can call forth new understandings and performances of their abilities and skills (Madigan 2011: 87).

Finally, mapping mutual influence helps couples see the ways they are embedded in relationships and systems of meaning beyond their control. This allows caregivers and the couples they seek to empower to continue to engage in cultural critique—critique that allows them to relate differently to cultural and social beliefs, attitudes, roles, and practices that sustain oppressive problems and passions in their lives.

In order to resist these oppressive forces actively and effectively, couples first must see, understand, and act on the power they have as a team to influence the problems they face. This is the focus of chapter 6, which looks at how a couple and its caregiver can attend to teamwork while facing the passion of contempt in the context of a new baby.

6

ATTENDING TO TEAMWORK

A couple that has hoped and planned for a new baby can experience great joy when an infant joins the family. But a new child also brings unique tensions to a couple—especially a young couple that has not been together for long. When a baby arrives, sleep deprivation, anxiety about the future, postpartum depression, a change of roles, and a myriad of other dynamics bring new, and often unexpected, pressures to a partnership (Rholes et al. 2001; Shapiro & Gottman 2005; Gottman & Gottman 2007). Ella and Sam are just beginning to understand this, three months after adopting newborn baby Cicely.

They have been married just three years, and now they are sitting around their kitchen table, sharing coffee with their pastor while Cicely sleeps in her bassinet. Pastor Jack has come for the third time to see how the partners are doing in their new roles as parents—and as a family rather than a couple.

"It's such a joy to watch you both care for Cicely, treating her like the precious miracle that she is," Jack said. "You seem to have changed so much—or maybe I'm seeing a side of you that I've not seen before."

"Oh, there are lots of changes!" Ella agreed.

"What's the biggest change been since Cicely became your daughter?" Pastor Jack asked.

"For me, it's just being so isolated," Ella answered. "I'm with her 24/7. I love her, and I love spending time with her, but it kind of feels like the rest of the world has gone on without me. I miss being at work, knowing what's going on, being around people."

"That sounds tough, honey," Sam said, rubbing her shoulder. He sighed. "For me, life has just totally turned upside down. I'm used to coming home from work and having Ella to myself. Usually there's dinner on the stove, and we've got a movie to watch or plans to go out. Now I have to do the cooking and the cleaning and the laundry and all that other stuff that Ella used to take care of. It's exhausting."

Ella rolled her eyes. "Oh, please, Sam," she said scornfully. She looked at Pastor Jack, shaking her head. "Poor little guy has to do his share around the house. Must be tough." Then she nodded at Sam for a few seconds before smiling gently. "Seriously, I appreciate everything you're doing. But do you have to be so dramatic about it? Can't Cicely be the center of attention for a while?"

"Uh oh," Pastor Jack said. "Remember when we talked about The Overwhelm and Judgment a couple of weeks ago? Sounds like they're back! Do we need to talk?"

Sam and Ella looked at each other. "That'd probably be a good thing," Ella said. "Last time you were here, it was helpful to see how bad those things make our life. But we're not doing so well at changing them."

A CLOSER LOOK AT THE PROBLEM AND THE PASSION

Ella's tone of voice, body language, and mocking words in response to Sam suggest that contempt—one of Gottman's (1999) Four Horsemen—is a spiritual passion affecting their relationship. Contempt—communication that seriously suggests one partner is superior to another—is one of the strongest predictors of divorce (ibid.) and a highly toxic behavior for any relationship. It is present when partners roll their eyes, belittle, and mock each other. Yet it can become a habitual way of relating for some couples. Pastor Jack has seen Sam and Ella express contempt before, and he is rightly concerned to eliminate it before Cicely is old enough to learn this way of communicating from her parents.

It's no surprise, either, that both Ella and Sam feel stressed by their new roles as parents. Most couples—67 percent, in fact—report less satisfaction with their relationship after the birth of a first child (Shapiro, Gottman, & Carrere 2000), and numerous studies suggest that the transition to parenthood can create a larger drop in relational satisfaction than almost any other factor (Belsky & Hsieh 1998; Kurdek 1999; Lawrence et al. 2008; Parade 2010; Sanders 2010; Twenge, Campbell, & Foster 2003; Wallace & Gotlib 1990; Crohan 1996). Partners who once (perhaps for years) could make each other the center of their worlds must suddenly accommodate a third person into their relationship—a tiny, needy person who demands their total attention, care, and nurture around the clock.

This means that in the weeks and months after a baby joins a family, parents spend less time relaxing together; they make fewer shared decisions; and they feel less connected emotionally and socially to their partners (Feeney et al. 2001). Housework and other chores increase exponentially, coping skills are pushed to their limits, and everyone is sleep deprived and chronically exhausted. Conflict increases by a factor of nine, the risk of depression and anxiety increases, stereotyped gender roles take over, fathers withdraw into work and career, and the couple nearly stops having sex and talking to each other in meaningful ways (Gottman & Notarius 2002). New parents feel underappreciated, neglected, and lonely; at the same time, there is more hostility at home; partners fight more; and there is less passion and less emotional connection than ever (Shapiro & Gottman 2005; Gottman & Gottman 2007). Women, especially, report higher levels of dissatisfaction in their marriages after the birth of a child (Cowan et al. 1991; Shapiro, Gottman, & Carrere 2000; Meijer & van den Wittenboer 2007); women are also at higher risk of depression, anxiety, chronic fatigue, and feelings of low self-esteem after the birth of a first child.

Under such conditions, it can be easier to fall into a cycle of criticism-defensiveness-contempt-withdrawal. This is one reason that it is imperative for spiritual caregivers to take the initiative in reaching out to new parents, identifying the Powers that are working against their sense of connectedness and agency, and attending to the teamwork that is present despite problems and passions such as contempt and overwhelm.

ATTENDING TO TEAMWORK VS. PROBLEM TALK

When faced with a large, seemingly insurmountable challenge to their relationship, most couples engage in "problem talk," telling a story about the difficulties the change has created for them. For example, new parents overwhelmed by the relational challenges introduced by an infant can celebrate the baby but otherwise focus on the problems they have with their partner: "She's so moody"; "He seems angry all the time"; "We never talk any more"; "We argue all the time." These totalizing accounts of their relationship dominate to such an extent that other possible stories about their life together—stories about their teamwork as parents, for example, or their ongoing connection as partners—remain unacknowledged, undeveloped, and untold.

Consider how Ella and Sam respond when Pastor Jack asks what has changed the most since their baby arrived. They could focus on the love that they feel for Cicely, their new identities as parents, or the shift from being a couple to being a family. But instead, Sam and Ella focus on what's been most difficult in the transition. In the excerpt below, problem talk is highlighted in **bold** type, with *explanatory notes* in italics:

Ella: For me, it's just **being so isolated**. I'm with her 24/7. I love her, and I love spending time with her, but it kind of **feels like the rest of the world has gone on without me. I miss being at work, knowing what's going on, being around people.** (*Here, Ella identifies and complains about her sense of isolation and being "left behind."*)

Sam: That sounds tough, honey. (*Sam acknowledges Ella's complaint with an empathic statement and rubs her shoulder to show he cares. This suggests he is building positivity in the relationship.*) For me, **life has just totally turned upside down. I'm used to coming home from work and having Ella to myself. Usually there's dinner on the stove, and we've got a movie to watch or plans to go out. Now I have to do the cooking and the cleaning and the laundry and all that other stuff** that Ella used to take care of. **It's exhausting.** (*Sam identifies a litany of complaints that could be heard as veiled criticism of Ella, as if he is blaming her for his increased work and exhaustion.*)

Ella: Oh, please, Sam. Poor little guy has to do his share around the house. Must be tough. (*Ella responds with contempt, rolling her eyes and mocking Sam.*) Seriously, I appreciate everything you're doing. (*A possible repair attempt.*) But **do you have to be so dramatic about it? Can't Cicely be the center of attention for a while?** (*Here Ella returns to problem talk by subtly indicting Sam for being dramatic and taking attention from the baby; these sorts of belittling comments are another example of contempt.*)

Problem talk of this sort solidifies the problems that the couple faces. It emphasizes the overpowering nature of the changes they are living through, and it recruits the people around them—friends, family members, coworkers—into performing the same, problem-saturated story. The more the couple rehearses the problematic narrative, the more powerful it becomes. This is why spiritual caregivers who have helped to externalize and map the influences of a problem or passion must take mapping one more step: they must map the influence of the couple *over* the problem.

This is different than mapping the couple's role in the life of the problem. Rather than identifying the ways in which the couple's thoughts, feelings, and actions help sustain or maintain the problem or passion, as discussed in chapter 5, mapping the couple's influence over the problem seeks to identify the ways in which the couple has overt agency in relation to the problem or passion. In the language of narrative psychotherapy, it is time to identify "sparkling moments" or "unique moments" when alternative stories are possible—stories in which the couple unites as a team to confront and stand firm before the problem or passion.

In order to attend to teamwork, a spiritual caregiver must carefully notice moments in the couple's story—past, present, or future—when there is evidence that they cooperated to resist the negative effects of the problem or passion at work to distance them. This is accomplished through ongoing mapping conversation that uses deconstructive and unique-outcome questions.

BEGINNING TO ATTEND TO TEAMWORK

In the process of mapping mutual influence, the spiritual caregiver and couple develop a thorough sense of the effects of the problem or passion—the ways that it works, overtly or covertly, to put distance between partners; the things that it says to introduce dissatisfaction or to coax certain, unhelpful behaviors; the ways it gets both partners to cooperate with its tactics so that it can continue its impish and destructive presence in their lives. Once the effects of the problem or passion are clearly seen, it is time to identify the ways in which the couple has resisted the problem's tactics, even a little bit, to assert the partners' own preferences for their life together. Identifying points of resistance helps couples see and claim their unique gifts and strengths that are to be named, protected, nurtured, and put to use through their partnerships.

We could describe these points of resistance as "gaps" in the problematic story (Madigan 2011)—thin openings through which the possibility of an alternative story line might be glimpsed, introduced, and developed. These sparkling moments are mostly unnoticed actions and intentions that interrupt problem talk, call its assumptions into question, or cause the dominant, problem-saturated story to swerve a bit. To be useful as possible alternative story lines, these sparkling moments or unique outcomes must be salient—that is, important or at least curiosity provoking—to the couple. Questions that help elicit these moments of resistance fall mainly along the axis of action, although axis-of-meaning questions can also be useful in identifying unnoticed intentions, preferences, values, and dreams that can be developed into accounts of teamwork and eventually into stories of partnership.

Questions that can help identify and attend to moments of teamwork include the following:

- Have there been times when you as a couple have been able to rebel against the problem or passion and satisfy some desires that it blocks? Did that bring you pleasure or displeasure? Why? (Madigan 2011: 89)
- Has there been a time when the problem or passion could have taken control of your relationship but didn't? (Freedman & Combs 1996: 125)
- Have there been times when you thought, even for a moment, that the two of you might step out of the prison created by the problem or passion? What did the landscape free of the problem or passion look like? (Madigan 2011: 89)
- How did the two of you escape from the problem or passion long enough to have this conversation today? How have you kept it at bay long enough to talk to me?
- Have the two of you ever stood up to some of the expectations put on you by the problem or the passion and decided to do something your own way instead? (Freedman & Combs 1996: 125)
- What do you think might have helped support the hope in yourselves that you could, someday, stand up to or slip away from the problem or passion? (Madigan 2011: 89)
- Can you imagine a time in the future when you might defy the problem or passion together and get a break from it?

(ibid.) What would that look like? What would the effects of that be for you as a couple?

- What kind of relationship would you like to have together with the problem or passion? (Nylund 2000: 110) Has there ever been a time when you've had something approaching that sort of relationship?
- Why hasn't the problem or passion totally convinced you as a couple that you have to settle for less in life? Do you see a future that is yours as a couple and not the problem's or the passion's? (ibid.)

It is important to remember that the purpose of these questions is to attend to teamwork between the couple. Occasionally, one partner will identify an act of resistance, a gap, or possible story line based on her or his own experience—something she has done, for example, or an intention he holds for the future. When this happens, it is important to inquire about the other partner's presence and role in that action, decision, or intention: How did your partner contribute to you standing up to the problem or passion in that way? What was it about your partner that allowed you to see that possibility? What do you need from your partner in order to do that again? This moves the moment of possibility from solo achievement toward teamwork. Individual accomplishments are important and should be celebrated, but the spiritual caregiver's primary goal at this point is to attend to instances of teamwork as a way of bringing the couple closer together despite the problem or passion that has been separating them.

EXPRESSING FONDNESS AND ADMIRATION

Feelings of separation and emotional distance can be one effect of stress in a relationship. In fact, many problems and passions thrive by reducing intimacy between partners. Notice, for example, that Ella doesn't acknowledge the unspoken emotions behind Sam's complaints and that she cannot receive his verbal and physical expressions of support. Likewise, Sam is unable to voice his complaints without making them sound like veiled criticisms of Ella. These interactions suggest that the couple is feeling out of touch with each other and perhaps out of sync with each other's feelings. This sort of emotional distance makes hostile interactions and expressions of contempt more likely.

The effects of contempt can be reversed, however, when partners express feelings of fondness and admiration for each other (Gottman 1999; Gottman, Gottman, & DeClaire 2006). "When couples make a full, conscious effort to notice things they like about each other's personalities and character, and to express that fondness right out loud, their relationships typically improve" (Gottman, Gottman, & DeClaire 2006: 114). On the other hand, if partners repeatedly replay negative thoughts about each, rehearsing old injuries and disappointments, the cycle of distance and isolation tends to perpetuate itself.

Spiritual caregivers can help nurture fondness and admiration in at least three ways. First, they can invite partners to identify and express three to five positive qualities that characterize each other's personalities. Once the partners have named the qualities that characterize each other, each explains their choices and tells the story of a specific incident in which their partner exhibited one of those qualities (Gottman 1999: 206).

Second, spiritual caregivers can invite partners to identify the three aspects of their relationship for which they are most thankful. Then they express their gratitude for those qualities, explaining what each means to them. For example, "I am grateful for how safe I feel when I am with you, because it allows me to take risks and trust that we will always be together." Partners can meditate on these thanksgivings during the day when they are apart from one another.

Finally, spiritual caregivers can invite partners to create their own "fondness and admiration checklist" that includes everything they value about their partner (Gottman 1999). John Gottman recommends that they memorize as much of their list as possible and rehearse it, or at least parts of it, daily. They should also express appreciation at least once daily for something their partner does, focusing on what their partner added to their lives. In the process, they should "make it a point to touch the partner (both verbally and physically) in a purely affectionate manner" (ibid., 209).

By practicing fondness and admiration on a daily basis, couples not only build behavioral habits that enhance their relationship, they also create a reservoir of goodwill that helps them weather inevitable conflicts and resist the temptation of contempt, which lures them to lash out at each other with belittling words and body language.

ATTENDING TO TEAMWORK WITH ELLA AND SAM

After Ella agreed that it would be helpful to revisit The Overwhelm and Contempt as forces that created difficulties for her and Sam, Pastor Jack briefly summarized what they had learned during their previous mapping conversation.

"If I remember right," he said, "one of the effects of The Overwhelm is that you start to feel distant from each other, and then you feel like you are competing to see who feels most overwhelmed. Once that starts, Contempt usually talks Ella into saying something that hurts Sam's feelings. Then Sam withdraws, and you both start to feel even further apart. And Sam, after you withdraw, you are apt to let Contempt talk you into criticizing Ella in your head and then out loud, directly to her. Did I get that right?" The couple nodded, watching him closely.

"I wonder," the pastor said, looking at them quizzically. "Has there ever been a time when The Overwhelm started to push you apart but you were able to resist it, even a little bit?" (*The pastor introduces a unique outcome question that invites the couple to identify a time on the axis of action when they took steps to resist the effects of the problem.*)

The partners looked at each other. "No, not . . . really," Sam said hesitantly. "It feels like it's been going on so long that it doesn't have to try very hard anymore." (*Mired in the problem-saturated story, the couple is unable to identify a gap or opening to a possible alternative story that includes their having agency in the face of the problem.*)

"Well," said Pastor Jack, "how about a time when The Overwhelm was keeping you apart but you were able to name your desire to be closer together?" (*The pastor tries again, this time using a unique-outcome question that assumes that the problem is in control but that the couple was able to act on the axis of meaning to state their desire to resist the problem.*)

"Yes," Ella said immediately. "Last weekend, Cicely was napping, and we were both sitting on the couch exhausted. Sam asked which chore we should tackle first, and then he said, 'Wouldn't it be great if we could just ignore the chores and relax together for an hour?' And I laughed and said, 'That would be wonderful.' And then he pulled me into a hug, and we just lay there for a little bit." (*Ella identifies a moment when Sam not only expressed a desire to resist the problem, but actually took action to bridge the distance between them when she expressed the same desire.*)

"Was that pleasant or unpleasant for you?" Pastor Jack asked. (*Not wanting to assume that this was a positive, salient moment for Ella, the pastor asks for the meaning that she ascribes to the event.*)

"It was wonderful," Ella said. "It felt like I had my husband back for a minute—like I knew we were in this together, and I was important to him, and we were more important than all the dishes and laundry and other stuff." (*Ella confirms that this was a positive, salient moment for her and goes on to make additional meaning about the action. She is beginning to widen the small gap she identified earlier; it is now a definite opportunity to develop an alternative story of the couple's influence over the problem and passion.*)

"It was good for me, too," Sam agreed. "I felt a little like we were skipping school or something—like we were playing hooky just because it was important to us. And I remember feeling her heartbeat while I held her. That was really nice." (*Sam also confirms that this was a positive, salient moment and goes on to make additional meaning about the event.*)

"What does it say about you as a couple that you were able to take that time to reconnect that way?" asked Pastor Jack. (*The pastor asks a question about identity, keeping to the axis of meaning that the couple has already been following.*)

"Probably that we were too tired to do anything else!" Ella laughed. Sam laughed with her. (*This moment of humor is a positive exchange between the couple.*)

"I think it shows that we knew it was important to connect with each other physically for a minute," Sam said. "That we knew we needed to prioritize each other at that moment." (*Sam continues to make meaning of the event, ascribing a certain wisdom to the couple. This wisdom can later be identified and developed as a particular gift or resource for which the couple has responsibility for stewardship.*)

"You knew your relationship with Ella was important enough to be a priority," the pastor affirmed. "What was it about her that helped you reconnect right then, Sam?" (*The pastor intentionally broadens the conversation to focus on the qualities of Ella that helped Sam make her a priority, strengthening the sense of the emerging story as a tale of teamwork.*)

"I don't know," Sam said. "She just looked so beautiful, and I realized how much I love her even though we've been really irritated with each other. And when I touched her, she sort of melted into me. She just felt 'open,' you know? Like she wanted to be touched or taken care of." (*Sam makes additional meaning about his relationship and response to Ella and her contributions to the unique outcome.*)

"I was tired," admitted Ella. "I wanted to be comforted. And it was like Sam picked up on that, even though he started out talking about the chores." (*Ella likewise makes additional meaning about the unique outcome and Sam's contribution to it.*)

"So even though you were surrounded by things that needed to get done, you were still attuned to each other's needs?" Pastor Jack asked. (*The pastor tentatively identifies another gift or resource that was present in the moment—attunement to one another's emotional needs.*)

"Yeah, I guess," Sam said. "I hadn't thought about it that way."

"Maybe it was being still and quiet for a minute that helped us tune in," Ella suggested. (*Ella identifies another resource—this time along the axis of action—that contributed to the unique outcome, naming a condition that the couple can intentionally recreate later.*)

The three sat in silence for a minute, letting the moment sink in. "Sounds like maybe you found a way to resist The Overwhelm and Contempt without even knowing you were doing it," Pastor Jack said quietly. "You came together as a team even when it was prodding you to separate and get busy." (*The pastor identifies the event as a moment of teamwork, underscoring its significance and highlighting the couple's agency in the moment.*)

This brief illustration of attending to teamwork, in which one narrow gap appears in the dominant story of the distance created by The Overwhelm, demonstrates the power of this stage of the SMART approach. Attending to teamwork, coupled with separating the couple from problems and passions and mapping the effects of those energies on the couple, can allow couples to see that the problem-saturated story is not the only story they can tell about their relationship—that no matter how much distance the problem or passion has put between them, there are moments (some large, some small) when they unite as a team to resist the effects of the problem or passion. The identification of a possible shared story of teamwork provides a platform on which to construct and expand a richer, fuller account of the couple's cooperative efforts to resist problems and passions. This process of reclaiming partnership is the next stage of the model.

TRY IT YOURSELF

Using curious questions to help couples identify their influence over problems and passions can be an empowering way of attending to teamwork. To experience the effects of mapping a person's influence over a problem or passion, explore the following questions for yourself. First, return to the quality about yourself that you identified in chapters 4 and 5 as causing dissatisfaction—the one that causes you mild discomfort from time to time. Every time you encounter a _____ in the questions, fill in the blank with the quality you have identified.

Map your influence over _____ by reflecting on these questions:

- Have there been times when you have been able to rebel against _____ and satisfy some desires that it blocks? Did that bring you pleasure or displeasure? Why?
- Has there been a time when _____ could have taken control of you or your relationships but didn't?
- Have there been times when you thought, even for a moment, that you might step out of annoyance created by _____? What did the landscape free of _____ look like?
- How did you escape from _____ long enough to read this chapter? How have you kept it at bay long enough to make it this far in your career?
- What was a time that you stood up to some of the expectations that _____ puts on you and decided to do something your own way instead?
- What do you think might have helped support the hope in yourself that you could, someday, stand up to or slip away from _____?

- Can you imagine a time in the future when you might defy
  _____ and get a break from it? What would that
  look like? What would the effects of that be for you?
- What kind of relationship would you like to have with
  _____? Has there ever been a time when you've
  had something approaching that sort of relationship with it?
- Why hasn't _____ totally convinced you that you
  have to settle for less in life? Do you see a future that is yours
  and not _____'s?

Take a deep breath. What feelings did these questions awaken
in you? How did they make you feel about your relationship to the
quality you identified? How hopeful are you after answering the
questions? Note the level of energy in your body and the sort of
self-talk going through your mind. Then take a short break—get
a drink of water, stretch, walk around the room a couple of times.

IMPLICATIONS FOR SPIRITUAL CARE
AND COUNSELING

When the challenges of a new baby and the destructive passion of
contempt come between a couple, a spiritual caregiver must move
nimbly to identify and attend to an alternative story about fondness, admiration, and teamwork. After externalizing and mapping
the effects of the problem and passion, the caregiver begins to
attend to teamwork by mapping the influence of the couple over
the problem and passion—looking at the times when the partners
have expressed agency in resisting or overcoming the Powers that
are coming between them. Simultaneously, caregivers focus on
helping the couple express fondness and admiration toward each
other. It is difficult for contempt to retain a stronghold in a relationship when the covenant friendship has a solid foundation of
turning toward one another with gentleness and expressing genu-
ine fondness and admiration for each other.

Attending to teamwork is an initial move in recreating partnership—that is, developing a new (or forgotten) story of the couple united as partners who are working together for the life they
prefer and value. By standing in solidarity with the couple toward
this vision and as an ally against the Powers, the spiritual caregiver

advocates for *enacting justice*, which, for pastoral theologian Sharon Thornton (2002), is analogous to the classical function of care as reconciliation. Justice, in this case, consists of an increasingly deliberate and critical move toward mutuality and partnership as norms for marriage and other covenant relationships.

Shifting from teamwork to partnership is a critical step in establishing a more just covenant friendship that can actively and effectively resist oppressive forces and passions. This is the focus of chapter 7, which looks at how a couple can be empowered to reclaim partnership. The context of chapter 7 is the spiritual passion of withdrawal, brought on by a partner's virtual affair through the Internet.

7

RECLAIMING PARTNERSHIP

Reclaiming partnership is the goal that spiritual caregivers aim for throughout the processes of externalizing problems and passions, mapping their influence, and tracking the agency that partners have in relation to the Powers that push them apart. As couples begin to story themselves as heroes, a team working valiantly together to resist and overcome problematic passions and powers, they reclaim the partnership that brought them into a committed, covenant relationship in the first place. In the process, they become active and empowered agents of the relational gifts, graces, and resources over which they have stewardship, learning to use those resources for their own benefit and for the benefit of others.

Partners Pat and Lynn, for example, are just beginning to identify those gifts, graces, and resources with the help of a licensed clinical social worker who has specialized training in spiritually integrative counseling. The couple sought help last month when Lynn discovered that Pat has been in an ongoing online relationship with a person whose screen name is "Duke." Although Pat maintains that Duke is just a close friend, Lynn sees the relationship as an emotional affair, if not infidelity. Lynn feels betrayed, angry, and hurt, as if Pat cannot be trusted.

They named the problem Betrayal; its primary effect is the spiritual passion of stonewalling, which dominated their communication in the weeks after the affair was revealed—Lynn regularly "exited" conversations by turning away from Pat and seeming not to hear or comprehend what was going on. When that happened, Pat withdrew, too, until they were both sitting as quietly as two stone walls.

In their previous session with the counselor, however, no stonewalling occurred. Instead, the couple talked about a time when they resisted the effects of Betrayal and stayed connected as a team—which left them feeling hopeful and energized. Today their counselor wants to help them begin to reclaim their partnership by moving their story as a couple from that solitary moment of teamwork toward an expanded sense of partnership.

"So, last time," the counselor begins, "we talked about a moment when Lynn came home and found Pat on the computer, but instead of withdrawing or feeling anxious, just said, 'Whatcha working on, babe?' And you, Pat, responded by saying, 'Come here and see,' rather than withdrawing or feeling like you were under surveillance."

"Right," Pat said. "It was like a moment when we both decided not to let Betrayal run our thoughts or our emotions. I noticed what Betrayal was saying to me, but I decided to ignore it."

"And instead of stonewalling, I decided to treat Pat like Betrayal had never shown up in our lives," Lynn added.

"So both of you made independent decisions about responding to Betrayal," the counselor said. The couple nodded. "But what about you as a couple—something that's true about you as partners—let you make those decisions, let you trust that it was okay to ignore Betrayal's voice and follow your own inclinations instead?"

Pat and Lynn looked at each other. "We've got a long history together," Pat said. "We've weathered a lot of tough times."

"We always make it through, no matter how hard it is," Lynn agreed. "We're great parents, we're best friends, and we never intentionally hurt each other."

"Great start," their counselor responded. "You're great parents, you're best friends, you never intentionally hurt each other, and you have a long history of making it through tough times. You know how to work together to keep things going."

"Yes," the couple said together.

"And we're going to make it through this," Lynn added. "No matter how much it hurts."

A CLOSER LOOK AT THE PROBLEM AND THE PASSION

Pat's online relationship with Duke—a combination of emotional intimacy and virtual sexual activity—represents a significant (and increasingly common) relational conflict in industrialized nations. More and more people are involved in online sexual activities (Daneback, Cooper, & Mansson 2005; Goldberg et al. 2008; Grov et al. 2011), which, like Pat's, can include an exchange of sexually stimulating words, images, or behaviors (an activity known as "cybering"; Subotnik 2007). When online activity violates agreements about sexual or emotional exclusivity, it becomes a cyber-affair—a violation that both men and women call infidelity (Henline, Lamke, & Howard 2007). Cyber-affairs should be taken as seriously as any marital infidelity; one study recorded separation or divorce in 22.3 percent of couples in which one partner experienced compulsive online sexuality (Schneider 2003).

Of course, online sexual activity rarely begins as a compulsion. It occurs on a continuum from benign curiosity (for example, conversation in a sexual chat room) to obsessive involvement and sexual addiction (for example, performing for others via webcam in real time) (Dryer & Lijtmaer 2007; Griffiths 2012). Access, affordability, and anonymity make online sexuality attractive and can lead to greater involvement (Griffiths 2012), until a participant develops a cyber-persona that values "techno-intimacy" over the risks of real intimacy (Dryer & Lijmaer 2007). When this happens, online sexual activities can begin to substitute for offline sex (Griffiths 2012).

Partners of those engaged in online sex often consider it to be sexual infidelity, emotional infidelity, or pornography use and thus an act of betrayal (Whitty 2003). Women and men agree that online infidelity is highly unacceptable (Helsper & Whitty 2010), and cyber-affairs can be as emotionally painful as a live affair. Being lied to repeatedly is a particular source of distress in cyber-affairs (Schneider 2003), and jilted partners feel a range of emotions from hurt, betrayal, rejection, abandonment, devastation, and loneliness to shame, isolation, humiliation, jealousy, and anger.

Stonewalling, Lynn's primary response to the cyber-affair, can accompany any of these emotional responses. Stonewalling happens when a person withdraws from an interaction. Instead of listening attentively, a stonewalling person looks down or away and stops offering verbal cues—"uh-huh," "okay," "yeah"—that show interest. The person's jaw or chin might become tight. A stonewalling person often feels flooded by strong emotion, and as a result the body's alarm system is going off—heart rate increasing, adrenaline flowing, breaths getting faster. Stonewalling is an effort to withdraw in order to self-soothe and calm the body (as discussed in chapter 4). Men tend to stonewall more than women (Gottman 1999).

As a spiritual passion, stonewalling becomes dangerous when it leads to emotional disengagement. When this happens, the withdrawal is so complete that partners stop connecting, positively or negatively. They seem to operate in parallel without affecting each other. Neither attempts to soothe the other, and there is little or no evidence of a covenant friendship. This is where Pat and Lynn were headed when stonewalling caused one and then the other to withdraw. It succeeded in putting so much distance between them that they could no longer connect at the level of covenant friendship. Each was becoming isolated from the other, and their distance was growing. It placed their entire relationship at risk.

RECLAIMING PARTNERSHIP
VS. ATTENDING TO TEAMWORK

To reduce the risk of further distance and separation, it is important that partners and their caregiver identify at least one moment of teamwork when the covenant friendship brings the couple closer together to resist the powers and passions that keep them stewing in isolation. Once that moment of teamwork is identified, it must be developed into a stronger narrative of shared identity, meaning, and agency so that the partners can begin reclaiming partnership. This is a process of inviting the couple to enrich and make sense of the story of teamwork as a counterpoint to the dominant, problem-saturated story ("We are no longer functioning as partners"). "Attending to teamwork" invites people to notice actions and intentions on the axis of action that contradict the dominant problem story (Madigan 2011); "reclaiming partnership" invites them to create a portion of a story that can be "held alongside the problem story as part of an emerging and coherent alternative narrative" (ibid., 89). This is largely accomplished through questions that explore the axis of meaning, accentuating identity and agency.

For example, notice how Pat and Lynn's counselor focuses on reclaiming partnership by asking about the meaning that the couple ascribes to the teamwork identified during the previous meeting. Discourse focused on identity, agency, and meaning are highlighted in **bold**, with explanatory notes in *italics*.

Counselor: So, last time, we talked about a moment when Lynn came home and found Pat on the computer, but instead of withdrawing or feeling anxious, just said, "Whatcha working on, babe?" And you, Pat, responded by saying, "Come here and see," rather than withdrawing or feeling like you were under surveillance. (*The counselor summarizes the salient moment from the previous session.*)

Pat: Right. It was like a moment when **we both decided not to let Betrayal run our thoughts or our emotions.** I noticed what Betrayal was saying to me, but **I decided** to ignore it. (*Pat makes meaning that highlights agency, naming actions and intentions that identify influence over the problem.*)

Lynn: And instead of stonewalling, **I decided** to treat Pat **like Betrayal had never shown up** in our lives. (*Lynn likewise highlights agency and positive intention.*)

Counselor: So both of you made independent decisions about responding to Betrayal. (*The counselor affirms the individual actions and intentions of each partner.*) But what about you as a couple—something that's true about you as partners—let you make those decisions, let you trust that it was okay to ignore Betrayal's voice and follow your own inclinations instead? (*Here, the counselor focuses on the identity of the couple, asking a question along the axis of meaning so that the partners can develop a shared sense of meaning and identity as a couple about the teamwork being explored. This is an overt move toward reclaiming partnership.*)

Pat: We've got a **long history** together. We've **weathered a lot of tough times.** (*Pat responds by articulating the couple's long history of partnership and their resiliency during tough times.*)

Lynn: We **always make it through**, no matter how hard it is. We're **great parents**, we're **best friends**, and we **never intentionally hurt each other.** (*Lynn reiterates the couple's resiliency and adds three other qualities that contribute to their identity as partners.*)

Counselor: Great start. You're great parents, you're best friends, you never intentionally hurt each other, and you have a long history of making it through tough times. You **know how to work together to keep things going.** (*The counselor reflects the couple's language about the past and adds a summary statement that contributes*

	additional meaning about the qualities of the partner-ship in the present.)
Couple:	Yes. (*The couple accepts the counselor's additional meaning.*)
Lynn:	And **we're going to make it through** this. No matter how much it hurts. (*Lynn adds an expectation about the couple's agency in the future, reclaiming partner-ship and extending it beyond the current crisis. Now partnership has been reclaimed in the past, present, and future.*)

Reclaiming partnership occurs as curious questions allow a couple to see their situation from many perspectives, moving from a thin description to a richer, more complex account of what is happening in their relationship. For example, Lynn and Pat had a dominant story of, "My partner betrayed me, I betrayed my partner, and we both withdrew." In counterpoint, after attending to teamwork they are reclaiming partnership through a story line that says, "Betrayal entered our partnership, and we are both capable of withdrawing, but we are resilient people, good parents, best friends, and we are going to make it through this despite the pain." This is a far more complex—though still incomplete—account of their situation. It is also an account that places their partnership, rather than their separation, at the cen-ter of the plot.

BEGINNING TO RECLAIM PARTNERSHIP

Spiritual caregivers begin to help a couple reclaim partnership by asking questions that can "flesh out" barely visible story lines about teamwork. These alternative story lines develop, grow, and take on a life of their own as spiritual caregivers introduce questions that invite people to imagine possibilities, explore their experiences, and "try out" different scenarios to see what fits. "People become curious about, and fascinated with, previously neglected aspects of their lives and relationships, and as these conversations proceed, these alternative storylines thicken, become more significantly rooted in history, and provide people with a foundation for new initiatives in addressing the problems, predicaments, and dilem-mas of their lives" (White 2007: 62).

So much of what we experience passes by without being woven into the primary story we tell about our lives. Our experiences become meaningful and important only to the extent that they become a part of the familiar and known stories of our lives (White 2007). Events, conversations, and observations that seem out of sync with those familiar stories pass through our consciousness without making a lasting impression and without shaping our sense of who we are or who we can be. Yet those experiences harbor potentially significant and meaningful consequences for our identities, relationships, values, understandings, and commitments. By helping couples identify and attend to these out-of-sync moments, allowing them to capture and retain the significance of such moments for their partnerships, spiritual caregivers can facilitate the unleashing of the potentiality of such experiences. This can allow couples to assume greater authorship of their lives as partners, reclaiming their shared commitments and giving voice to what they intend and value for their future.

A variety of questions can help accomplish the reclaiming of previously ignored experiences (see Madigan 2011: 89–95). They include the following:

- How were you able to get yourselves to work, to school, and to church and thereby defy the problems and passions that want to keep you to themselves?
- Given everything that the problem and passion have going for them, how have you objected to the way it pushes you around as a couple?
- How might you stand up to the problem or passion's pressure to come between you again? How might you refuse its requirements of you?
- How might your presence here today, together, be a type of radical disobedience to the problem or passion?
- What does this tell you about yourself as a couple that you otherwise would not have known?
- By allowing yourselves to work as a team a bit, do you think you are in any way becoming more of a partnership? How?
- Where do you think you will go next, now that you have embarked on reclaiming partnership as a couple?
- Is this a direction you see yourself taking in the days, weeks, and years to come?

- How do you think it is likely to revive your relationship, restore your friendships, or renew your vitality as a couple?
- Is this your preference for the best way for you to live as a couple? Why?
- Do you see this as a good or bad thing for you as a couple? Why?

Questions that facilitate a couple's reclaiming partnership help elicit new understandings and awarenesses, primarily along the axis of meaning. Such questions invite people actively to construct and identify positive qualities about their partnerships that can become preferred values, intentions, and ways of living for the future. Often, couples who engage these sorts of questions discover aspects of their lives together that had not yet been articulated, named, or storied; these aspects, brought to life through curious inquiry, can become important threads for new stories about the value, meaning, and power of a partnership as the couple faces a future free of the influence of particular problems and passions. Reclaiming partnership can move a couple's shared story in new directions, promising a different outcome than they might have predicted prior to talking with a spiritual caregiver. Such is the creative power of the SMART approach.

EXPANDING COGNITIVE SPACE

No matter how much creative power the SMART approach brings to the process of reclaiming partnership, the mind of each partner also has a role to play. Specifically, each partner must expand the "cognitive space" allotted to information about the other and about the relationship—the part of the brain that holds details about the partner's history, daily routines, likes, dislikes, and so forth (Gottman, Gottman, & DeClaire 2006), as well as about the way the couple met, their first impressions, their dating history, and so forth (Gottman 1999). (This is sort of like allocating space on a hard drive for particular data files.)

Couples who carry and remember accurate and detailed information about each other—what Gottman (1999) calls "love maps"—tend to have happier relationships and to cope better with life's difficulties: "People who make these maps can tell you the name of their partner's friends, what their partners worry about, what their partner's current stresses are, and their partner's hopes, aspirations, and life dreams" (ibid., 81). Creating cognitive space for each other is about being known and feeling known (ibid., 161).

To create cognitive space after an important life event or transition, marriage therapists John Gottman and Julie Gottman recommend that couples ask each other the following questions (2006: 95–96) at a relaxed pace, taking time to listen and respond in open and supportive ways:

- How has this event (change, transition, loss, stress) changed how you feel about your life?
- How has it changed the way you feel about your role in your extended family?
- How has it changed the way you feel about your job?
- How have your priorities changed since this event occurred?
- How has it changed your views regarding religion, spirituality, or God?
- How has it changed the way you think about the future?
- How has it changed the way you think about serious illness or death?
- How has it changed your experience of time? Are you more concerned or less about what might happen in the future? Do you find you're paying more attention or less to things that are happening in the present moment?
- How has it changed your relationship with your friends or relatives?
- How has it changed what you need for yourself?
- How has it changed your sense of security in the world?
- How has this affected your daily mood?
- What kind of support do you need from me as your enter this period of your life?

Facilitating the expansion of cognitive space that each partner allots to the other can be an important way for spiritual caregivers to support and sustain efforts to reclaim partnership. It is far easier to reclaim partnership when each partner feels known and cherished than when one or both has the sense of being a stranger to the other.

RECLAIMING PARTNERSHIP WITH LYNN AND PAT

As Lynn and Pat began creating a more complex account of themselves as partners, one that moved Betrayal and Withdrawal out of the center of the story, the cognitive space they allotted to their relationship naturally started to expand. In the process, their counselor was able to use curious questions to continue to enrich the previously ignored, out-of-sync moment toward a possible alternative story about reclaiming partnership.

"So that afternoon when Lynn came home and found Pat on the computer—the moment when you both told Betrayal to take a hike, so to speak—that fit who you are as partners?" the counselor asked. (*The counselor asks a question on the axis of meaning, seeking to identify whether the moment of teamwork is a preferred way of being for the couple, one that ought to be developed further as a possible alternative story line.*)

"Yes, I think so," Lynn said. "It fit who we are as friends—trusting, able to work through our differences, nondefensive (most of the time, anyway!)." (*One partner affirms the out-of-sync moment as a preferred way of being, naming additional attributes that it suggests about the partnership.*)

"It definitely fit," Pat agreed. "That's the way I want to be with Lynn—an open book, not sneaking around and keeping secrets. I totally meant what I said: 'Come and take a look and see what I'm up to here. I've got nothing to hide.'" (*The other partner also affirms the preferred status of the out-of-sync moment, adding even more attributes to the growing list of positive qualities about the partnership.*)

"What does this tell you about yourself as a couple that you wouldn't otherwise have known?" the counselor asked. (*The counselor asks another question along the axis of meaning to elicit a richer account of the partnership; the question invites the couple to make additional meaning about the out-of-sync moment and its implications for their partnership in the present and future.*)

"It tells me we can recover pretty quickly," Lynn said. "That even when I'm hurt, I can still choose to trust Pat—and that I can trust that Pat will know what I need to feel secure, like being invited to come over and look at the computer screen without having to ask." (*Lynn adds meaning related to the relationship's resilience, to the cognitive dimension of trust, and to the ability of the partnership to elicit feelings of security.*)

"It tells me that we're on the same wavelength," Pat added. "That even though we can shut down when things get intense, we're pretty good about getting through things when we keep it casual—that we both know what the other needs when we don't make a big deal out of it." (*Pat adds meaning about the partners' intuitive understandings of each other and about their unique way of approaching their problems—theirs is a casual rather than formal approach to conflict resolution.*)

"Right," added Lynn. "When we come at things head-on, Betrayal knows how to keep us apart. But if we sneak up on it, we can outsmart it every time. No matter what the 'experts' say about how things should happen, we know what works for us." (*Lynn further affirms the couple's conflict-resolution style, affirming the "local knowledge" vested in the partners and their innate wisdom about outsmarting the problem and the passion that created distance.*)

"How does that affect your partnership?" the counselor asked. (*The counselor asks a question that could lead the partners along the axis of action or meaning, depending on how they interpret it.*)

"It makes us stronger," Pat said. (*Pat uses the question to define the partnership as "stronger" than prior to the cyber-affair.*)

"I agree," added Lynn. "It shows us that together we're stronger than whatever happened to push us apart—that our friendship and commitment to each other will carry us through, that we know each other so well, we know what it will take to heal from this." (*Lynn agrees with the meaning that Pat contributed, adding the concept of "healing" to the qualities of the relationship.*)

"Have you thought of your partnership as 'healing' before?" asked the counselor. (*The counselor asks directly about the concept of "healing" as a way of checking to see if this is a story line that the partners find helpful and preferable to the dominant story they have been telling about the effects of the cyber-affair.*)

"No," said Lynn, "but I like the sound of that." (*Lynn voices intrigue about the idea of the partnership as one that is "healing."*)

"It makes sense," Pat said. "Together, we are good medicine. Apart, we keep causing pain." (*Pat accepts the meaning and names the partners as "medicine" for each other. With this conversational move, the couple is well on the way toward reclaiming partnership.*)

This short illustration of reclaiming partnership, in which a couple enriches one moment that is out of sync with the dominant story into a possible alternative—and quite contradictory—plotline suggests the power of the fourth stage of the SMART approach. Reclaiming partnership—accomplished after separating the couple from problems and passions, mapping mutual influence, and attending to teamwork—allows a couple to tell a new story about their relationship, a story in which the Powers have much less influence over the well-being of the partners and their life together. The process of telling this new story is the final stage of the approach and the focus of the next chapter.

TRY IT YOURSELF

Developing alternative story lines empowers couples to reclaim partnership in the midst of problems and passions. To experience the effects of identifying and enriching out-of-sync experiences into alternative story lines, explore the following questions for yourself. First, return to the quality that you identified in chapters 4 through 6 as causing dissatisfaction—the thing about yourself that causes mild discomfort from time to time. Every time you encounter a _____ in the questions, fill in the blank with the quality you have identified.

Begin developing an alternative story to the dominant narrative about _____ by reflecting on these questions:

- How are you able to function at work, at school, during worship, and thereby defy the effects of _____?
- Given everything that _____ has going for it, what are some ways you have objected to or resisted the way it pushes you around?
- How might you stand up to _____'s pressure in the future? How might you refuse its requirements of you?
- What do these things tell you about yourself (and your relationship to _____) that you otherwise would not have known?
- By allowing yourself to relate differently to _____, do you think you are in any way becoming more of the person you want or were created to be? How? What difference does that make to you?
- Of all the people in your life who might confirm this newly developing picture of yourself? Who might have noticed this first?

- Who would support this new understanding of yourself?
- Who would you most want to notice?
- Where do you think you will go next, now that you have embarked on reclaiming your life from _____?
- Is this a direction you see yourself taking in the days, weeks, and years to come? Why or why not?
- How do you think you are likely to revive your relationships, restore your friendships, or renew your vitality as you relate differently to _____?
- Is this your preference for the best way for you to live? Why?
- Do you see this as a good or bad thing for you? Why?
- Do you consider this to your advantage and the disadvantage of _____, or to the advantage of _____ and your disadvantage? Why?
- Given your expertise in the ways of _____, what have you learned about it that you might want to warn others about?
- As a veteran of _____ and all that the experience has taught you, what strategies would you recommend to others struggling with the same situation?

Now take a deep breath. What feelings did these questions awaken in you? How did they make you feel in relation to the quality that you identified? How hopeful are you after answering the questions? What seems possible or probable now, as compared to prior to reflecting on the questions? Note the level of energy in your body and the sort of self-talk going through your mind. Then take a short break—get a drink of water, stretch, walk around the room a couple of times.

IMPLICATIONS FOR SPIRITUAL CARE AND COUNSELING

Despite the heartbreak of a cyber-affair, the spiritual passion of stonewalling could not prevent a couple from reclaiming partnership when they set themselves to the tasks of expanding cognitive space for each other and enriching out-of-sync moments that challenged the dominant story of hurt, pain, and emotional distance. After externalizing, mapping effects, and attending to teamwork, the spiritual caregiver begins to reclaim partnership by asking questions that stimulate the couple's curiosity about a moment that does not fit the dominant story. At the same time, caregivers help the couple develop complex maps of their relationship and of each other's psychological worlds, expanding the cognitive space devoted to knowledge about one another and the relationship. It is difficult for stonewalling and withdrawal to sustain themselves where a covenant friendship has a rich repository of accurate, detailed information about the partners to sustain it through difficult times.

Recreating partnership leads naturally to telling a new story of the couple united as partners, working together for the life they prefer and value. Standing in solidarity with the couple through this process, the spiritual caregiver is both an ally against the Powers and one who *enacts justice* as an advocate for mutuality and partnership as critical norms for marriage and other covenant relationships.

Shifting from reclaiming partnership to telling a new, shared story is a vital step in solidifying a justice-oriented covenant friendship that can actively and effectively resist oppressive forces and passions. This is the focus of chapter 8, which looks at how a couple can work with a spiritual caregiver to identify and recruit audiences for their new story of mutuality and partnership. The context of the work in the next chapter is the spiritual passions awakened when one partner retires, creating a crisis for the couple.

8

TELLING A NEW STORY

Married for thirty years, Jim and Irma raised five children (three from his first marriage, two from hers), navigated two careers, and had a generally satisfying life together. Then Jim's job retired him at age sixty-five, while Irma, sixty, continued working.

Jim felt useless at home. It bothered him that Irma was the primary breadwinner, and he stewed alone all day about being forced to retire. When Irma came home, he took out his frustration on her. For nine months, the demons of Uselessness and Contempt did their best to tear the couple apart. But in the past sixty days, with the empowerment of their pastor, the couple has managed to reclaim partnership and strengthen their covenant friendship. Now the problem and passion have little influence over their daily interactions.

Unfortunately, their children and friends don't know that. They still walk on eggshells around the couple, repeating the stories about the tension caused by the retirement. Fewer people drop by for a visit, and Jim's friends have stopped inviting him on Saturday fishing trips at the lake. Their children only want to talk to Irma on the phone. Everyone expects an argument when Irma and Jim are together.

It's time for Irma and Jim to tell their new postretirement story to others with clarity and consistency so that their family and community can help make it a reality rather than continuing to perpetuate—unwittingly—an old, problem-saturated story about conflict. This chapter explores how that can happen.

A CLOSER LOOK AT THE PROBLEM

The months- or years-long transition from working life to retirement can be a time of financial strain, relational conflict, depression, gender-role reversals, and other challenges. This is especially true after the recent financial setbacks around the globe, as a growing number of couples retire in more precarious financial positions than they intended. Nonetheless, most researchers agree that retirement represents a relatively mild change in a couple's relationship, one that poses little threat to long-term marital quality (Atchley 2001). Of course, what happens as a person or couple adjusts to retirement can be quite subtle (Davey & Szinovacz 2004); it varies from person to person, and each partner experiences the retirement differently (Van Solinge & Henkens 2005). For most couples, retirement is a positive experience; for some, negative; for many, neutral. But no matter how retirement is experienced, most adjustment problems afterward are brief in nature (Atchley 2001).

Still, some factors can make the transition to retirement more difficult. For example, people who have a strong attachment to work—those who have held a particular job for a long time, for example, or who are deeply invested in their current position; those who have little control over the timing of retirement (like Jim); those who are very anxious about the meaning of retirement; and those who feel little personal power—are likely to find it more difficult to adapt to retirement (Van Solinge & Henkins 2005). Self-esteem, advance planning, and health also affect adjustment to retirement (Reitzes & Mutran 2004). Gender, however, seems to make little difference; women and men respond similarly to retirement (ibid.).

Overall, couples seem to fare better when both partners retire at the same time. When one partner is retired but the other is not—like Irma and Jim—the couple tends to report less satisfaction with their relationship; this is especially true when the husband is retired but the wife is working (Chalmers & Milan 2005). Retired couples who have adult children living at home also report less satisfying relationships. Married people tend to be especially unhappy if their retirement gives their working partner more influence or power, as Jim's retirement did for Irma (Szinovacz & Davey 2005).

It is rarely retirement itself, however, that determines how satisfying a relationship or a life becomes when a career ends. Rather, retirement satisfaction must be looked at in the context of overall relational satisfaction (Atchley 2001). A couple's problems, passions, and level of satisfaction before retirement are likely to continue after retirement. This is why it is important that spiritual caregivers empower couples, long before retirement approaches, to enhance their covenant friendships, express fondness and admiration, learn to accept mutual influence, build strong and effective partnerships, and resist spiritual passions as a team. Maintaining a strong covenant friendship allows partners to continue to tell a positive couple story about their relationship—and every story needs an audience, both to keep it fresh and to help keep it alive by retelling it to others.

TELLING A NEW STORY, IMAGINING AUDIENCES

Stories are curious things. They take on lives of their own as they are told and retold from person to person, community to community, and audience to audience. Stories about relationships are no different: they require an audience to come alive and convey their full meaning. Learning a couple's story is how others—friends, family, children, communities—appreciate, learn from, support, retell, and build on the stories of partnerships. In the process, audience members identify the qualities of a couple's life that they want to adopt for their own partnerships. They also find ways to carry into the future the values and commitments of couples they admire, creating an ongoing legacy. Performing the stories of our partnerships for others, then, becomes a way of shaping the futures of our communities. As a couple begins telling a new story about a reclaimed and empowered partnership, creating yet another account of the improved quality of their covenant friendship, it is important that they perform that meaning publicly for others who can help the story become stronger, take on new meaning, and grow into the future.

Retelling the new story unfolds as the couple imagines multiple audiences who can hear and receive their emerging story. The more audiences available for a new story, the stronger and more powerful it is likely to become. White (2007) identifies four benefits of telling new stories to carefully chosen audiences. These audiences provide opportunities, he writes, for people who are restorying their lives to do the following:

- Reappear on their own terms in the eyes of community members and in the eyes of the outsiders who were invited to participate
- Experience an acknowledgment of the identity claims expressed in their stories
- Experience the authentication of these identity claims

- Intervene in the shaping of their lives in ways that were in harmony with what was precious to them (184)

Couples begin to imagine potential audiences when the spiritual caregiver asks perspective-shifting questions that invite partners to imagine how the new story might affect the people around them. These questions help a couple identify potential audiences that can receive, witness, appreciate, and help perform emerging accounts of empowered and empowering partnership. As the new story is told and retold to these audiences, it becomes realized—made tangible, palpable, and brought to bear on daily life (Bidwell 2004b). In the account above, Irma and Jim's pastor has failed to help them retell their new story to their friends and children, which makes it more difficult to counter the negative story that started at Jim's retirement. They need a wider audience to help sustain their new story!

BEGINNING TO TELL A NEW STORY

A number of narrative strategies can help people tell and retell new stories to a variety of audiences. Some of these approaches entail delicate ethical and relational negotiations in order to prevent harm; therefore, they require specialized training. Three of these practices, however, are appropriate for spiritual caregivers who work in faith communities, specialized ministries, and other settings. The first practice is inviting the couple to identify audiences and retell their story on their own. The second is inviting audiences to participate in celebrations and rites of passage that document the new story in public ways. The third is making the couple a consultant to other partners who are in similar situations.

Inviting the Couple to Identify Audiences
and Retell the Story

The easiest and most effective way to identify audiences and to tell and retell new stories is to have the couple do it themselves. This happens not through overt invitation or suggestion, but simply through questions that raise the possibility of talking to others about their new story. The partners will decide on their own whether, and to whom, to tell the new story. The spiritual caregiver's task is to help them identify possible audiences, imagine how those audiences might respond to the new story, and reflect on what it would be like to share the new story. The initiative, freedom, and responsibility for telling the new story beyond the helping conversation belong to the couple.

Questions that help couples identify potential audience members and consider whether to tell them new stories include these:

- Who should celebrate this change with you? What would it mean to them (and to you as a couple) to know what's different in your relationship? How could you let them know?
- Who needs to be brought up to date about the changes in your relationship? What difference would it make to you if they knew? How would that person knowing about the changes support this new knowledge about you as a couple?
- Who would have predicted that you would overcome your problem and passion? What did they know about you that let them make this prediction? What would they say about this development in your relationship? How could you share with them the strategy you used to renew your partnership?
- How could you let others know about your new story as a couple? Who should know first? How might they respond? How will you tell them? What will it mean to you for others to be aware of the changes you've made?
- Who would be pleased by the ways you have changed your relationship to the problem and the passion? What should they know about it?
- Who would appreciate the ways in which you have strengthened your partnership? What would they find most inspiring? How would they support you?
- Of all the people in your life who might confirm this newly developing picture of the two of you working together as partners, who might have noticed this first? How did they notice? What would you like to say to them?
- Who would you most want to notice these changes?

Spiritual caregivers do not actually have to suggest talking with a potential audience member; it can be useful simply to identify potential audience members from the past, present, or future, from the couple's life or from public life (such as political figures or celebrities). Doing so can help couples feel connected and supported, reminding them of the network of resources in which they are embedded (Freedman & Combs 1996).

Inviting Audiences to Celebrate

A second way to recruit an audience and begin to circulate a couple's new story is to invite selected people to a celebration or rite-of-passage ceremony. This occurs as partners near the end of their work with a spiritual caregiver. The event can include some form of documentation—a certificate, for example, or a letter from the spiritual caregiver—that acknowledges the accomplishments of the couple. The celebration or ceremony introduces the new story to people who are important to the couple so that it can begin to flow into a wider circle of supportive friends and relatives.

As partners near the end of their work with a spiritual caregiver, the caregiver can ask, "In our final meeting together, how would you like to celebrate the changes you have made—the ways you have overcome the problems and passions that overwhelmed you, the ability to work together as a team, the reclaiming of your partnership? Are there two or three people who should be here to celebrate with you?"

If the couple chooses, two or three friends, family members, coworkers, or other audience members can be invited to the final meeting for a celebration or rite-of-passage designed collaboratively by the couple and the spiritual caregiver. Reviewing the progress of the couple, which may include the partners giving an account of their new story of empowered partnership, should be a significant part of the process.

That final conversation could also include a renewal of marriage vows, signing a new covenant, establishing a formal mission statement for the relationship, telling the story of how the partners overcame the problems that oppressed them, giving an account of what new strengths and values they had discovered in each other, and so forth. The caregiver could write a letter summarizing the process of change and highlighting the strengths of the couple; the caregiver could also prepare a certificate to recognize the couple's accomplishments—for example, "Masters at Slaying Jealousy and Strife" or "Committed Covenant Partners." Be creative—as caregiver, you can and should document what the couple is proudest of achieving. This document can be a touchstone for the couple when tough times appear in the future.

Making Consultants of Couples

Serving as consultants to other troubled relationships can be a final way that empowered couples retell their new stories to others. This does not mean that empowered couples actually *meet* with others, but that they document their experiences for the benefit of others. Spiritual caregivers can invite successful couples to write letters or make digital recordings for other troubled partnerships that might seek help from the caregiver in the future; in these consulting documents, empowered couples offer advice, support, and strategies for overcoming similar problems and passions. The documents can have creative titles, such as, "Jim and Irma's Field Guide to Getting Along after Retirement." With the couple's permission, the spiritual caregiver can share these documents with future couples seeking care.

SHARED VALUES AND MEANINGS

Telling and retelling their new story is one of the ways partners solidify shared values and meanings, a mainstay of the covenant friendship. Shared values and meanings develop as partners bring their life dreams together, merging their goals, activities, and stories, and creating rituals between themselves—such as shared meals, a hug and kiss in the morning, holiday traditions, or playful jokes (Gottman 1999: 106). This dimension of a covenant partnership provides the emotional reservoir that sustains a couple through difficult times. From it flow the positive interactions, fondness, and admiration necessary for the successful resolution of conflict. Thus it is important that spiritual caregivers attend to meaning and values as they empower couples.

Shared meaning and values emerge from at least four areas of a couple's life. Gottman (1999) describes these as:

- *Rituals:* This includes a broad range of shared activities, from daily routines such as dinnertimes and running errands to annual events such as religious holidays and family vacations.
- *Roles:* Wife, husband, son, daughter, doctor, homemaker, student, dancer, etc.
- *Goals:* These tangible markers involve both short- and long-term aspirations: from working out four times a week, to owing [sic] a home, to getting an advanced degree or a raise in salary, to becoming a grandparent.

- *Symbols:* These involve the intangible existential ponderings around the fundamental question, What is the *meaning* of . . . home, family, love, trust, autonomy, dependence, ad infinitum.

Few couples reflect intentionally on the symbolic, metaphorical, and existential dimensions of their relationships. As a result, they sometimes tell rather thin stories about shared meanings and values. To build a shared sense of meanings and values, John Gottman and his colleagues suggest that partners ask each other the following questions (over time, not all at once!):

- What goals do you have in life, for yourself, for our marriage, for our children? What would you like to accomplish in the next five to ten years?
- What is one of your life dreams that you would like to fulfill before you die?
- We often fill our days with activities that demand immediate attention. But are you putting off activities that are great sources of energy and pleasure in your life? What are those activities?
- Who are we as a family in the world? What does it mean to be a _____ (insert your family's last name)?
- What does the idea of "home" mean to you? What qualities must it have? How is this like or unlike the home where you grew up?
- How important is spirituality or religion in your life? How important is it in our marriage and in our home? How is this like or unlike the home where you grew up?
- What's your philosophy of how to lead a meaningful life? How are you practicing (or not practicing) this philosophy?
- What rituals are important to you around mealtimes?
- What rituals are important to you around holidays?
- What rituals are important to you around various times of day (getting up, leaving the home, coming home, bedtime, etc.)?
- What rituals are important when somebody in our family is sick?
- How do we get refreshed and renewed? How do we relax?
- What rituals do we have around vacations?
- What does it mean to be a husband or wife in this family?

- What does it mean to be a mother or father in this family?
- How do you feel about your role as a worker?
- How do you feel about your role as a friend? As a relative? As a member of our community?
- How do we balance the various roles we play in life? (Gottman, Gottman, & DeClaire 2006: 267–68)

Inviting couples to write a mission statement for their relationship can be an effective way to document shared meanings and values. It is especially useful as "homework" between conversations with the spiritual caregiver. Caregivers can suggest that a couple write, in twenty-five to fifty words, a statement of purpose for their partnership. It should include adjectives that describe the qualities they want to display to others—respectful, loving, playful, flexible, and so forth.

In the next conversation with their spiritual caregiver, the couple can explore the statement, describing what it says about them and elaborating on the meaning of each phrase. I have seen partners carry these mission statements in their wallets, hold each other accountable for behaviors inconsistent with their mission statements, and make family decisions based on the mission and values expressed in such statements. These documents can be a powerful tool for communicating shared meanings and values.

Being intentional about nurturing a couple's shared meanings and values not only strengthens the covenant friendship. It also provides a richer background for the new story the couple has been empowered to tell, weaving it into a larger narrative about the shared dreams, aspirations, and commitments of the partners—a story predicated on their own choices and preferences rather than on sociocultural stories being told about them or that they accept uncritically. This richer background provides a more confident position from which to recruit audiences and perform preferred stories about mutuality, empowerment, and partnership.

TELLING A NEW STORY WITH IRMA AND JIM

After worship one Sunday, Irma and Jim joined their pastor for lunch at a local diner.

"We've been doing a lot better after you helped us out," Irma said. "But our kids and our friends don't seem to notice it. It's like they expect us to still be fighting. They treat Jim like he's going to explode at any minute." (*Irma outlines the ongoing effects of the old, problem-saturated story.*)

"It's getting pretty old," Jim admitted.

"I wonder," the pastor said. "Do you think anyone else has gotten the news about the changes the two of you have made?" (*The pastor subtly introduces the idea of a larger audience for the new story.*)

"Well, I think they'd notice it if they paid attention," Jim said.

"But, baby—I don't think they *are* paying attention," Irma laughed.

The pastor took a sip of iced tea. "Who in your life needs to be brought up to date about the way you two have changed since Uselessness and Contempt stopped controlling your relationship?" (*The pastor asks overtly about recruiting audiences for the new story.*)

"The kids, definitely," Irma said. (*Irma identifies one potential—and preferred—audience.*)

"My fishing buddies," added Jim. (*Jim identifies another potential and preferred audience.*)

"And our closest friends," Irma suggested. Jim nodded. (*The couple expands potential audiences.*)

"What will be different for you when your children, your fishing buddies, and your closest friends know how much better things have gotten?" the pastor asked. (*The pastor asks a question on the axis of meaning, encouraging the couple to imagine how it would affect them to intentionally tell the new story to others.*)

"I don't know," Irma said. "I just think things would feel more relaxed again. We'd laugh more and spend more time together." (*Irma responds on the axis of action.*)

"They'd see that I'm not just a grumpy old man," Jim laughed. "They'd know that Irma and I are still the partners we've always been." (*Jim responds on the action of meaning.*)

"And what would that mean to you?" the pastor asked. (*The pastor follows Jim's lead, asking another question on the axis of meaning.*)

"It would mean our friends and our family know who we really are," Jim said. "That we haven't changed just because I retired—that I'm still the same guy that loves his wife and sticks by her and works things out. We're still a team." (*Jim makes six statements of meaning: the couple would be known for whom they are; the couple hasn't changed after retirement; he loves his wife; he sticks by his wife; he works things out; and the couple is a team. This could be significant meaning-making that enriches the new story of empowered partnership, and it is made possible by the thought of sharing that story with others. Jim's response emphasizes acknowledgment and authentication of the couple's preferred identity as one of the primary benefits of telling the new story to their selected audience.*)

"It would mean we could all be family again," Irma said. "It feels almost like we lost our kids last year because we argued so much. I want them to know it's safe to come home—that mom and dad are okay, and we're here for them again, just like we were when they were growing up." (*Irma makes five statements of meaning: the family can reunite; the couple can recover their children; home will be safe; the couple is okay; and the couple is available to their children as in the past. Like Jim's statement, this could be significant meaning-making to enrich the new story, made possible by sharing that story with others.*)

"Sounds pretty powerful," the pastor said, nodding. "I'd say it's pretty important that all of these folks get the message. How could you bring them up to date?" (*The pastor affirms the couple's meaning-making and asks a future-oriented question along the axis of action: How could they perform the new story for their preferred audiences in ways that would lead to the outcomes they have described?*)

"I think we should have a party, like we used to do," Jim said, "a Sunday afternoon barbeque. Invite 'em all over for ribs and potato salad and baked beans, play some good music. And then when everyone's having a good time, we can thank 'em." (*Jim names an approach that is congruent with their pre-retirement story; it is contextually appropriate and reflects the couple's values.*)

"That's a great idea!" Irma exclaimed. "We can thank them for being so supportive and tolerant of us while we got used to being a semi-retired family. Maybe we can even toast them—celebrate them for sticking with us until we got back on track." (*Irma builds on Jim's idea, adding the idea of celebrating the audience's strength and the resources they made available to the troubled couple.*)

"That sounds great!" the pastor said, grinning. "How do you think they'll respond?" (*The pastor invites the couple to imagine the effects on the audience of performing their new story in this way. It is a question on the axis of meaning.*)

"I imagine everybody will be pretty happy," Jim said. "I hate the thought that I chased them away by the way I acted, but I'd love to have 'em all back." (*Jim offers a thin account of how the party would affect the audience, then slips into a problem-saturated story that makes him the source of strife.*)

"You didn't chase them away, baby," Irma said, looking into Jim's eyes. "Uselessness and Contempt did that. And we're the one's calling them all home—together." (*Irma rejects Jim's account of himself as the cause of the tension, externalizing the problem and the passion. Then she names a new theme in the couple's story of empowered partnership: The couple taking the initiative to call their friends and family home—being a source of reconciliation rather than separation.*)

This short illustration of telling the new story, in which a couple identifies potential audience members, makes meaning in relation to sharing the story and identifies strategies for performing the new story in contextually appropriate ways, suggests the ripple effect of the fifth stage of the SMART approach. Telling the new story not only solidifies the changes made by the couple; it also initiates associated changes in their communities as the effects of their new narratives shape the stories that others are telling. Telling the new story—accomplished after separating the couple from problems and passions, mapping mutual influence, attending to teamwork, and reclaiming partnership—allows a couple to march confidently into the future, surrounded by communities of support.

Supportive community is an important theme for faith traditions around the world; community becomes a spiritual resource that can sustain (and hold accountable) partnerships that are mutual and empowering. It is essential that spiritual caregivers link couples to an ecology of care represented by supportive community. In community and a broader social ecology, couples have access to resources and wisdom not available within their partnership. They are also able to link their story of empowered partnership to larger community stories that support it, as well as to sacred stories that give it meaning, values, an ultimate context, and a hopeful horizon for the future.

TRY IT YOURSELF

Telling your new story to different audiences helps to make it real and to sustain it despite powerful cultural and personal stories that might stand in opposition to it. To experience the effects of identifying audiences and considering the effects of sharing your story, explore the following questions for yourself. First, return to the quality that you identified in chapters 4 through 7 as causing dissatisfaction—the thing about yourself that causes mild discomfort from time to time. Every time you encounter a _____ in the questions, fill in the blank with the quality you have identified.

Begin developing an alternative story to the dominant narrative about _____ by reflecting on these questions:

- Who should celebrate with you the ways you have learned to overcome _____? What would it mean to them (and to you) to know what's different in your relationship with _____? How could you let them know?
- Who needs to be brought up to date about the changes in your relationship with _____? What difference would it make to you if they knew? How would that person support this new knowledge about your changed relationship to _____?
- Who would have predicted that you would overcome _____? What did they know about you that let them make this prediction? What would they say about this development? How could you share with them the strategy you used to overcome _____?
- How could you let others know about your new relationship to _____? Who should know first? How will they respond? How will you tell them? What will it mean to you for others to be aware of the changes you've made?
- Who would be pleased by the ways you have changed your relationship to _____? What should they know about it?
- Who would appreciate the ways in which you have changed your relationship to _____? What would they find most inspiring? How would they support you?

Now take a deep breath. What feelings did these questions awaken in you? How did they make you feel in relation to the quality that you identified? How hopeful are you after answering the questions? What seems possible or probable now, as compared to prior to reflecting on the questions? Note the level of energy in your body and the sort of self-talk going through your mind. Then take a short break—get a drink of water, stretch, walk around the room a couple of times.

IMPLICATIONS FOR SPIRITUAL CARE
AND COUNSELING

Empowering couples to subvert the problems and passions in their relationships through a narrative approach to spiritual care can be effective and transformative. But it is not sufficient to end the caring process when the couple has reclaimed partnership. The caregiver must gently lead the couple toward telling their new story to preferred audiences. The communal sharing of the new story has two values for the couple: it solidifies the shared meanings and values inherent to the new narrative, and it results in public recognition and validation of their preferred identity as a couple. But the process of sharing the new story also has great value for the audience as well.

Our personal stories are sustained in community and embedded in larger communal narratives told by families, racial-ethnic groups, faith traditions, and cultural groups. When couples tell their stories to representatives of these larger communities, they convey, affirm, subvert, celebrate, resist, and embrace the bigger stories in which the story of their partnership is embedded. This adds to communal stories in important ways, shaping the future of all who hear the couple's new account of their relationship. It generates options, new possibilities, for others who may find pathways toward living more fully into preferred ways of being that are congruent with their own values, meanings, commitments, and beliefs. This ongoing telling and retelling of stories—individual stories, stories of partnership, communal stories, sacred stories— stories woven into a wondrous web of connection, is holy work; it can make us whole (and wholly holy, too).

EPILOGUE

If caring for the generations is a normative function of Christian partnerships and families, then working to empower couples could be among the most important activities of spiritual caregivers. By providing couples with tools to resist spiritual passions and oppressive cultural discourses, attending to teamwork, and reclaiming partnership, caregivers cultivate both the private and public dimensions of covenant relationships. Such empowerment allows couples to strengthen and sustain the covenant friendship that enables them to care effectively for themselves, the generation before, and the generation after in ways that promote mutuality, respect, equal regard, and relational justice. Thus the spiritual care provided to couples can influence multiple generations of biological, adoptive, or chosen family.

The approach to care proposed in *Empowering Couples* brings unique resources to this work. Caregivers who attend to the three dimensions of relational balance (behavioral, physiological, and interpretive) and to systemic and sociocultural influences (which manifest through spiritual passions and The Powers That Be) are more likely to provide holistic care to couples—"care of the soul" as classically understood in the Christian traditions. This is something that narrative psychotherapy, Gottman's approach to marital therapy, and desert spirituality cannot accomplish on their own. But brought together, they create a strong and flexible structure that can shelter couples and caregivers alike.

By weaving spiritual, scientific, and narrative wisdom into care that promotes mutuality, empowerment, equal regard, and relational justice, caregivers can become agents of Spirit who participate in the ongoing creation and repair of the web of being. This sort of anticipatory and participatory action can itself become a spiritual practice and discipline, and the spiritual and theological norms proposed in this text can be touchstones for care that is faithful (that is, trusts in the liberation that makes us whole), effective, and oriented toward justice.

NOTES

Introduction

1. The category "committed partnership" includes, but is not limited to, marriage. Many people assume that a legal, civil marriage—probably blessed by a religious leader if not formally established through a public ceremony in a religious context—is the norm for couples in committed, covenanted relationships. But this text uses the phrases "committed, covenanted partnerships," "committed, covenanted relationships," and variations on that theme to refer to any couple in which partners think of themselves as family, both those who are allowed to access the privileges of marriage through a legally binding relationship and those who cannot or do not, including same-sex partners, domestic partners, couples who are living together without legal status, and other configurations of coupledom. It is important to make this clear, because legal marriage remains the only form of covenanted partnership that is officially condoned and recognized, implicitly or explicitly, by many faith communities, and at this time only a handful of state governments recognize same-sex marriages or domestic partnerships. (To my knowledge, the only U.S. American faith communities who officially allow or endorse same-sex unions and marriages are the Metropolitan Community Church, the Unitarian-Universalist Fellowship, the United Church of Christ, some dioceses of the Episcopalian Church, and Reform Judaism.) Yet caregivers routinely encounter couples who are not legally married.

2. I am drawing here on the psychological concept of the "good-enough mother" developed by psychoanalytic psychiatrist Donald F. Winnicott, a pediatrician and an originator of object-relations theory; see Winnicott 1964/1992.

3. All language for God, or for divine or ultimate reality, is metaphorical; therefore, I use "Spirit" to refer as inclusively as possible to the transcendent dimension of life. I hope that readers and practitioners from a variety of religious and spiritual traditions, theistic and nontheistic, will find this practice hospitable. To use "the Spirit" or "the Holy Spirit" would more accurately reflect my own Christian identity but bring an unnecessarily exclusive tone to the text.

4. For more detail on the classical forms or functions of pastoral care, see Seward Hilter, *Preface to Pastoral Theology* (Nashville: Abingdon, 1958), and William A. Clebsch and Charles R. Jaekle, *Pastoral Care in Historical Perspective* (Englewood Cliffs, NJ: Prentice-Hall, 1964).

5. The term *Semitic* refers to the Afro-Asiatic ethnic, cultural, and language groups of Southwest Asia and Northeast Africa. The area is often referred to as the "Middle East," but that geographic designation only makes sense if you are located in a European context or in the Western Hemisphere. I use it here to designate the regions where Judaism, Christianity, and Islam originated, influence, and were informed by African traditional religions, Hellenistic thought, and other indigenous spiritual traditions.

6. See David H. Jensen, "What Do Presbyterians Say about Marriage?" in *Frequently Asked Questions about Sexuality, the Bible, and the Church: Plain Talk about Tough Issues*, ed. Ted A. Smith (San Francisco: The Covenant Network of Presbyterians, 2006), 59–62.

Chapter 2

1. I am using the term "covenant friendship" instead of Gottman's "marital friendship" (1999), which he defines in part as each partner's feeling of knowing and being known by the other, the awareness that each has of the other's psychological world, the level of fondness and admiration partners express for each other, and how often partners turn toward each other (rather than away) during nonconflict situations.

Chapter 3

1. It is also influenced by solution-focused and collaborative psychotherapies, two other postmodern approaches that share a social constructionist theoretical orientation.

2. It is unrealistic to expect a couple to live a problem-free life. Not only are human beings finite creatures who will always bump up against the limitations that create friction between them, but Gottman's research suggests that 69 percent of stable marriages experience perpetual problems—"issues with no resolution that the couple has been dealing with for many years" (1999: 96). The trick with such stubborn issues is to establish a way of staying in gentle dialogue about the problem rather than reaching gridlock. I believe a narrative approach to spiritual care helps achieve precisely that by teaching couples to have a mutual, shared conversation as a team allied against the problem rather than as individuals pushed apart by it.

Chapter 5

1. For more on narrative questions, including the sources of the mapping questions in this chapter, see Madigan (2011: 87–88), Nylund (2000: 90–91), and Freedman & Combs (1996: 68, 120–39).

REFERENCES

Almeida, David M., Katherine A. McGonagle, Rodney C. Cate, Ronald C. Kessler, & Elaine Wethington. 2002. "Psychosocial Moderators of Emotional Reactivity to Marital Arguments: Results from a Daily Diary Study." *Marriage and Family Review* 34, nos. 1/2: 89–113.

Anderson, Herbert. 2009. "A Spirituality for Family Living." In *Spiritual Resources in Family Therapy*, ed. Froma Walsh, 2nd ed., 194–211. New York: Guilford.

Ashford, Jose B., Craig W. LeCroy, & Dan C. Lortie. 2006. *Human Behavior in the Social Environment: A Multidimensional Perspective*. 3rd ed. Pacific Grove, CA: Thomson Brooks.

Atchley, Robert C. 2001. "Retirement and Marital Satisfaction." In *Families in Later Life: Connections and Transitions*, ed. Alexis J. Walker, Margaret Manoogian-O'Dell, Lori McGraw, & Diana L. White, 187–90. Thousand Oaks, CA: Pine Forge.

Belsky, Jay, & Kuang-Hua Hsieh. 1998. "Patterns of Marital Change during the Early Childhood Years: Parent Personality, Coparenting, and Division-of-Labor Correlates." *Journal of Family Psychology* 12: 511–28.

Bianchi, Suzanne M., & Melissa A. Milkie. 2010. "Work and Family Research in the First Decade of the 21st Century." *Journal of Marriage and Family* 72 (June): 705–25.

Bidwell, Duane R. 2001. "Maturing Religious Experience and the Postmodern Self." *Pastoral Psychology* 49, no. 4: 277–90.

———. 2004a. *Short-Term Spiritual Guidance*. Creative Pastoral Care and Counseling series. Minneapolis: Fortress Press.

———. 2004b. "Real/izing the Sacred: Spiritual Direction and Social Constructionism." *The Journal of Pastoral Theology* 14: 59–74.

Blevins, John B. 2005. "Queer as This May Sound: Toward New Language and New Practices in Psychology, Theology and Pastoral Care." Unpub. PhD diss. Atlanta: Emory University.

Bondi, Roberta C. 1987. *To Love as God Loves: Conversations with the Early Church*. Minneapolis: Fortress Press.

Breazeale, Kathlyn A. 2008. *Mutual Empowerment: A Theology of Marriage, Intimacy, and Redemption*. Minneapolis: Fortress Press.

Browning, Don S. 2003. *Marriage and Modernization: How Globalization Threatens Marriage and What to Do about It.* Kindle ed. Grand Rapids: Eerdmans.

———. 2010. *Reviving Christian Humanism: The New Conversation on Spirituality, Theology, and Psychology.* Theology and the Sciences. Minneapolis: Fortress Press.

———, Bonnie Miller-McLemore, Pamela Couture, K. Brynolf Lyon, & Robert L. Franklin. 1997. *From Culture Wars to Common Ground: Religion and the American Family Debate.* Louisville: Westminster John Knox.

Brussat, Frederic, & Mary Ann Brussat. 2010. "Be Like the Mountain: The Practice of Equanimity." *Spirituality and Practice: Resources for Spiritual Journeys.* http://www.spiritualityandpractice.com/practices/features.php?id=17965.

Buehler, Cheryl, Ambika Krishnakumar, Gaye Stone, Christine Anthony, Sharon Pemberton, Jean Gerard, & Brian K. Barber. 1998. "Interparental Conflict Styles and Youth Problem Behaviors: A Two-Sample Replication Study." *Journal of Marriage and the Family* 60, no. 1: 119–32.

Bureau of Labor Statistics (BLS). 2011. "American Time Use Survey—2010 Results." Washington, DC: United States Department of Labor. http://www.bls.gov/news.release/archives/atus_06222011.htm.

Chalmers, Lee, & Anne Milan. 2005. "Marital Satisfaction During the Retirement Years." *Canadian Social Trends* (Spring): 15–17.

Chinula, Donald M. 1997. *Building King's Beloved Community: Foundations for Pastoral Care and Counseling with the Oppressed.* Cleveland: United Church Press.

Clebsch, William A., & Charles R. Jaekle. 1964. *Pastoral Care in Historical Perspective.* Englewood Cliffs, NJ: Prentice-Hall.

Coontz, Stephanie. 2006. *Marriage, A History: How Love Conquered Marriage.* New York: Penguin.

Cowan, Carolyn Pape, Philip A. Cowan, Gertrude Heming, & Nancy B. Miller. 1991. "Becoming a Family: Marriage, Parenting, and Child Development." In *Family Transitions,* ed. Philip A. Cowan and M. Hetherington, 79–110. Hillsdale, NJ: Lawrence Erlbaum Associates.

Crohan, Susan E. 1996. "Marital Quality and Conflict across the Transition to Parenthood in African American and White Couples." *Journal of Marriage and Family* 58: 933–44.

Daneback, Kristian, Al Cooper, & Sven-Axel Mansson. 2005. "An Internet Study of Cybersex Participants." *Archives of Sexual Behavior* 34: 321–28.

Davey, Adam, & Maximiliane E. Szinovacz. 2004. "Dimensions of Marital Quality and Retirement." *Journal of Family Issues* 25: 431–64.

Demacopoulos, George E. 2006. *Five Models of Spiritual Direction in the Early Church.* Notre Dame, IN: University of Notre Dame Press.

Dryer, Joy A., & Ruth M. Lijtmaer. 2007. "Cyber-Sex as Twilight Zone between Virtual Reality and Virtual Fantasy: Creative Play Space or Destructive Addiction?" *Psychoanalytic Review,* 39–61.

Feeney, Judith A., Lydia Hohaus, Patricia Noller, & Richard P. Alexander. 2001. *Becoming Parents: Exploring the Bonds between Mothers, Fathers, and Their Infants.* New York: Cambridge University Press.

Fincham, Frank D. 2003. "Marital Conflict: Correlates, Structure, and Context." *Current Directions in Psychological Science* 12, no. 1: 23–27.

Foster, Richard J. 1988. *Celebration of Discipline: The Path to Spiritual Growth.* Rev. and exp. ed. San Francisco: HarperSanFrancisco.

Freedman, Jill, & Gene Combs. *Narrative Therapy: The Social Construction of Preferred Realities.* New York: Norton, 1996.

Galinsky, Ellen, James T. Bond, Stacy S. Kim, Lois Backon, Erin Brownfield, & Kelly Sakai. 2005. *Overwork in America: When the Way We Work Becomes Too Much.* Executive Summary. New York: Families and Work Institute.

Goldberg, Peter D., Brennan D. Peterson, Karen H. Rosen, & Mary L. Sara. 2008. "Cybersex: The Impact of a Contemporary Problem on the Practices of Marriage and Family Therapists." *Journal of Marital and Family Therapy* 34: 469–80.

Gottman, John M. 1999. *The Marriage Clinic: A Scientifically Based Marital Therapy.* New York: Norton.

———, & Julie S. Gottman. 2007. *And Baby Makes Three: The Six-Step Plan for Preserving Marital Intimacy and Rekindling Romance after Baby Arrives.* New York: Three Rivers.

———, Julie S. Gottman, & Joan DeClaire. 2006. *Ten Lessons to Transform Your Marriage.* New York: Three Rivers.

————, & Clifford I. Notarius. 2002. "Marital Research in the 20th Century and a Research Agenda for the 21st Century." *Family Process* 41: 159–97.

Graham, Larry K. 1992. *Care of Persons, Care of Worlds: A Psychosystems Approach to Pastoral Care and Counseling.* Nashville: Abingdon.

Griffiths, Mark D. 2012. "Internet Sex Addiction: A Review of Empirical Research." *Addiction Research and Theory* 20: 111–24.

Grov, Christian, Brian J. Gillespie, Tracy Royce, & Janet Lever. 2011. "Perceived Consequences of Casual Online Sexual Activities on Heterosexual Relationships: A U.S. Online Survey." *Archives of Sexual Behavior* 40: 429–39.

Hammer, Leslie, & Cynthia Thompson. 2003. "Work-Family Role Conflict." *Sloan Network Encyclopedia.* Boston: Sloan Work and Family Research Network.

Helsper, Ellen J., & Monica T. Whitty. 2010. "Netiquette within Married Couples: Agreement about Acceptable Online Behavior and Surveillance between Partners." *Computers in Human Behavior* 26: 916–26.

Henline, Branden H., Leanne K. Lamke, & Michael D. Howard. 2007. "Exploring Perceptions of Online Infidelity." *Personal Relationships* 14: 113–28.

Hilter, Seward. 1958. *Preface to Pastoral Theology.* Nashville: Abingdon.

Jensen, David H. 2006. "What Do Presbyterians Say about Marriage?" In *Frequently Asked Questions about Sexuality, the Bible, and the Church: Plain Talk about Tough Issues,* ed. Ted A. Smith, 59–62. San Francisco: The Covenant Network of Presbyterians.

Johnson, Kristen L., & Michael E. Roloff. 1998. "Serial Arguing and Relational Quality: Determinants and Consequences of Perceived Resolvability." *Communication Research* 25, no. 3: 327.

Kurdek, Lawrence R. 1999. "The Nature and Predictors of the Trajectory of Change in Marital Quality for Husbands and Wives Over the First 10 Years of Marriage." *Developmental Psychology* 35: 1283–96.

Lawrence, Erika, Alexia D. Rothman, Rebecca J. Cobb, Michael T. Rothman, & Thomas N. Bradbury. 2008. "Marital Satisfaction across the Transition to Parenthood." *Journal of Family Psychology* 22: 41–50.

Lester, Andrew D. 1995. *Hope in Pastoral Care and Counseling.* Louisville: Westminster John Knox.

———, & Judith L. Lester. 1998. *It Takes Two: The Joy of Intimate Marriage.* Louisville: Westminster John Knox.

Lewis, Jerry M. 2000. "Repairing the Bond in Important Relationships: A Dynamic for Personality Maturation." *American Journal of Psychiatry* 157: 1375–78.

Lian, Tam Cai, & Lim Siew Geok. n.d. "A Study of Marital Conflict on Measures of Social Support and Mental Health." *Sunway Academic Journal* 5: 97–110.

Madigan, Stephen. 2011. *Narrative Therapy.* Theories of Psychotherapy series. Washington, DC: American Psychological Association.

Madsen, William C. 2007. *Collaborative Therapy with Multi-Stressed Families.* 2nd ed. Guilford Family Therapy series. New York: Guilford.

McAdams, Dan P. 1993. *The Stories We Live By: Personal Myths and the Making of the Self.* New York: Guilford.

Meijer, Anne Marie, & Godfried L. H. van den Wittenboer. 2007. "Contribution of Infants' Sleep and Crying to Marital Relationship of First-Time Parent Couples in the 1st Year after Childbirth." *Journal of Family Psychology* 21: 49–57.

Miguez, Nestor, Joerg Rieger, & Jung Mo Sung. 2009. *Beyond the Spirit of Empire: Theology and Politics in a New Key.* Reclaiming Liberation Theology series. London: SCM.

Mitchell, Kenneth R. 1990. "Guidance, Pastoral." In *Dictionary of Pastoral Care and Counseling,* ed. Rodney J. Hunter, 486. Nashville: Abingdon.

Monk, Gerald, John Winslade, Kate Crockett, & David Epston, eds. 1997. *Narrative Therapy in Practice: The Archeology of Hope.* San Francisco: Jossey-Bass.

Neuger, Christie Cozad. 2001. *Counseling Women: A Narrative, Pastoral Approach.* Minneapolis: Fortress Press.

Nylund, David. 2000. *Treating Huckleberry Finn: A New Narrative Approach to Working with Kids Diagnosed with ADD/ADHD.* San Francisco: Jossey-Bass.

Osiek, Carolyn, & David L. Balch. 1997. *Families in the New Testament World: Households and House Churches*. Family, Religion, and Culture series. Louisville: Westminster John Knox.

Parade, Stephanie H. 2010. "Marital Satisfaction across the Transition to Parenthood: A Vulnerability-Stress-Adaptation Perspective." Unpub. PhD diss. Greensboro, NC: University of North Carolina.

Patton, John, & Brian H. Childs. 1988. *Christian Marriage and Family: Caring for Our Generations*. Nashville: Abingdon.

Payne, Martin. 2006. *Narrative Therapy: An Introduction for Counsellors*. 2nd ed. London: Sage.

Presbyterian Church (USA). 1993. *Book of Common Worship*. Louisville: Westminster John Knox.

Ray, Rebecca, & John Schmitt. 2007. *No-Vacation Nation*. Washington, DC: Center for Economic and Policy Research.

Regnerus, Mark. 2012. "Good News and Bad News in Marriage and Divorce Statistics." *Patheos*, May 14. http://www.patheos.com/blogs/blackwhiteandgray/2012/05/marriage-and-divorce-statistics/.

Reitzes, Donald C., & Elizabeth J. Mutran. 2004. "The Transition to Retirement: Stages and Factors That Influence Retirement Adjustment." *The International Journal of Aging and Human Development* 59: 63–84.

Rholes, W. Steven, Jeffry A. Simpson, Lorne Campbell, & Jami Grich. 2001. "Adult Attachment and the Transition to Parenthood." *Journal of Personality and Social Psychology* 81: 421–35.

Sanders, Kayla M. "Marital Satisfaction across the Transition to Parenthood." Unpub. MS thesis. Lincoln, NE: University of Nebraska. http://digitalcommons.unl.edu/sociologydiss/2.

Schnarch, David. 2009, 1997. *Passionate Marriage: Keeping Love and Intimacy Alive in Committed Relationships*. New York: Norton.

Schneider, Jennifer P. 2003. "The Impact of Compulsive Cybersex Behaviours on the Family." *Sexual and Relationship Therapy* 18: 329–54.

Shapiro, Alyson F., & John M. Gottman. 2005. "Effects on Marriage of a Psycho-Communicative-Educational Intervention With Couples Undergoing the Transition to Parenthood, Evaluation at 1-Year Post Intervention." *The Journal of Family Communication* 5: 1–24.

————, John M. Gottman, & Sybil Carrére. 2000. "The Baby and the Marriage: Identifying Factors That Buffer against Decline in Marital Satisfaction after the First Baby Arrives." *Journal of Family Psychology* 14: 59–70.

Subotnik, Rona. 2007. "Cyber-Infidelity." In *Infidelity: A Practitioner's Guide to Working with Couples in Crisis*, ed. Paul R. Peluso, 169–90. New York: Routledge/Taylor & Francis.

Szinovacz, Maximiliane E., & Adam Davey. 2005. "Retirement and Marital Decision Making: Effects on Retirement Satisfaction." *Journal of Marriage and Family* 67: 387–98.

Taylor, Charles W. 1999. *Premarital Guidance*. Creative Pastoral Care and Counseling series. Minneapolis: Fortress Press.

Thornton, Sharon G. 2002. *Broken Yet Beloved: A Pastoral Theology of the Cross*. St. Louis: Chalice.

Twenge, Jean M., W. Keith Campbell, & Craig A. Foster. 2003. "Parenthood and Marital Satisfaction: A Meta-Analytic Review." *Journal of Marriage and Family* 65: 574–83.

Van Solinge, Hanna, & Kene Henkens. 2005. "Couples' Adjustment to Retirement: A Multi-Actor Panel Study." *The Journal of Gerontology* 60: S11–S20.

Von Stutzman, Stephen. 2008. "Marital Conflict: A Comparison of Cross-Ethnic Adolescent Outcomes." PhD diss. Provo, UT: Brigham Young University.

Wallace, P. M., & I. H. Gotlib. 1990. "Marital Adjustment During the Transition to Parenthood: Stability and Predictors of Change." *Journal of Marriage and the Family* 52: 21–29.

Walsh, Froma, 2009. "Religion, Spirituality, and the Family: Multifaith Perspectives." In *Spiritual Resources in Family Therapy*, ed. Froma Walsh, 2nd ed., 3–30. New York: Guilford.

White, Michael. 2007. *Maps of Narrative Practice*. New York: Norton.

————, & David Epston. 1990. *Narrative Means to Therapeutic Ends*. New York: Norton.

Whitty, Monica T. 2003. "Pushing the Wrong Buttons: Men's and Women's Attitudes toward Online and Offline Infidelity." *CyberPsychology and Behavior* 6: 569–79.

Wimberly, Edward P. 1979. *Pastoral Care in the Black Church*. Nashville: Abingdon.

Wink, Walter. 1998. *The Powers That Be: Theology for a New Millennium*. New York: Doubleday.

————. 1992. *Engaging the Powers: Discernment and Resistance in a World of Domination.* Minneapolis: Fortress Press.

Winnicott, Donald F. 1964/1992. *The Child, The Family, and the Outside World.* Boston: Da Capo.

Ziegler, Phillip, & Tobey Hiller. 2001. *Recreating Partnership: A Solution-Oriented, Collaborative Approach to Couples Therapy.* New York: Norton.

INDEX